THE JOE DIAL

THE JOE DIAL

Master Your Life by Knowing the Three Kinds of People

JOE SCOTT

FRIENDESHA MEDIA INC.

Friendesha Media Inc.

ISBN 978-0-9833456-0-2
Printed in the United States of America by BookPrintingRevolution.com.
Dial graphic (book cover and interior) and Ladder of Life graphic designed by Joe Scott.

Library of Congress Control Number:
2011922463

Dedication & Thanks

This book is dedicated to my five children, Ryan, Daniel, Rebecca, Summer, and John, and to the future generations they will produce. May it help and protect them always. May it also help and protect you, the reader, and your future generations. I purposely made this book a hardcover so it would last for many years, and put the Dial on the cover to serve as a constant visual reminder of the ideas herein.

I want to thank God for giving me the life, the energy, the time, and the wealth of experiences to write such a book. I would also like to thank my editor, Andy Wolfendon, for all of his help and for the great work he did to finally get this book published, and Mariah Parker, the artist, for bringing my Joe Dial design to life so beautifully.

Thank You,
Your Common Man and Father of Five,
Joe

Contents

Welcome!

I'm not a big fan of Prefaces, Forewords, and Introductions. The way I see it, if an author has something to say, he should stick it in the meat of the book. So that's what I've done here. I won't waste your time with filler and prep-talk.

The only thing I *do* want to say, up front, is thanks for having a read. Though I originally wrote this book for my own kids and grandkids, it is meant for you and your family, too. If you like what you see here and think it makes sense, please pass it down and keep it around. Share it with your spouse, your kids, and your grandkids.

The Joe Dial isn't written for academics. It's written for the common man (and woman). But then, I believe we're *all* the common man. My fondest hope is that these words will eventually be translated into every language on Earth. Why? Not because I think the whole world should listen to me, but because I think the "wisdom" contained in these pages is important stuff that you already know in your heart. It's not my property or my product; it's just basic truth. And the truth belongs to all of us — like a natural resource.

I hope you'll use this book if you're looking for a better way to get along with your boss or co-workers, a new way to talk to your kids, or just some help in moving your marriage or friendships to a better place. *The Joe Dial* is a simple, no-nonsense guide to cutting through the complexities of human relationships and finding peace. May you use it in wisdom and good health.

1

Why Me and Why This Book?

My name is Joe. Guess you probably figured that out from the title. Yep, Joe is the name my parents slapped on me (not in a fit of creative inspiration, I'll admit), but I also fit the image of "a Joe" in many ways — as in "regular Joe," "just a Joe," "cup of Joe," "working Joe." I am a construction guy, with my very own hard hat. Joe the Builder, that's me. In fact, I thought about using that name in the book title, but it seemed a bit too hokey. Plus, I didn't want to be confused with that other Builder — you know, the little animated one with the talking bulldozer. I really do build things, though. I have had the honor and privilege of working in the construction business since I was literally eight years old. I *make* stuff for a living — great big, heavy stuff. You wouldn't mistake me for a Sven or a Norman.

I don't have a string of letters after my name, and I'm never, ever going to be invited to give a guest lecture on "Cognitive Biases in Psychological Research Studies" at the local think tank. I'm not someone who hides out behind walls of abstract ideas. I prefer to be out there in the nuts-and-bolts world, where ideas either produce measurable results or not. I don't have a pile of theoretical research to back up the ideas I'm about to share with you. Any wisdom I may have accumulated has come from dealing with real people in real situations.

My credentials are not those of a Harvard professor, but I believe I could teach many a Harvard professor a thing or two. How could I suggest such a thing?

Because I haven't *learned* my lessons from a book, I've *lived* them. I've field-tested them in the trenches, *literal* trenches, in many cases.

I was an average student in high school, with A's in math and gym; B's, C's, and D's in everything else. I dropped out of accounting college in my first year, then, at age twenty, I went into business for myself. I started with only a $150-a-month payment on a Ford F250 pickup truck and a toolbox. That was thirty-eight years ago. I've managed to stay in business through the recessions of '74 to '80, '89 to '96, '99 to '03, and finally the one from '07 to who-knows-when. All those years, I've paid every bill put in front of me. I've never used the excuse of a bad economy, a tough divorce, slow business, or someone else being late paying *me* to tell someone, "Sorry, I can't pay you now."

As for the skills I do have, I'm a master carpenter and master mason. I'm also a journeyman roofer, welder, mechanic, plumber, electrician, glazier, sheet metal man, drywaller, tile man, concrete finisher, steel erector, equipment operator, hydraulics engineer, sewer and water man, septic system installer, road and sidewalk builder, paver, and professional building estimator. Of course, I'm a builder, too — oh, and a licensed tractor-trailer driver. I'm also an unlicensed architect, accountant, lawyer, realtor, contract negotiator, banker, and sociologist. In my spare time (ha!), I'm a thirty-five-year scuba diver, boat captain, fisherman, lobsterman, and licensed pilot rated through multi-engine jet (own one too).

So, street smarts I have. Academic credentials? Not so much. Then what am I doing writing a book, and why should you bother reading it?

Not Your Average Joe

Well, I guess you may have gathered that in many ways, I'm *not* your average Joe. For one thing, I own a successful multi-million-dollar construction and development company, a position I wouldn't have gotten to without following the advice in this book. I've employed thousands of people over the years. I'm not easily pigeonholed when it comes to social class. I'm as comfortable talking to a forklift operator as I am to the president of a multinational corporation. During my busiest building years, you might have found me hashing over job specs with carpenters and masons at six in the morning, and then wining and dining banker friends till late in the evening. In my journey from the cold-water flats of my boyhood neighborhood to the three cozy zip codes where I now get my mail, I've had a chance to study thousands of people, of all nationalities, colors, cultures, creeds, and economic classes, in situations that tend to bring out the very best and the very worst. I'd say I've dealt with a lot more people in a lot more revealing circumstances than "the average Joe."

This is not just because of the work I do; it's because of the personality I happen to have. In case you can't already tell, I'm a big-time extravert. I like to meet people and mix things up. I like face-to-face encounters. I like to look people in the eye and hear their honest opinions spoken in their own voices. I like to watch their body language.

Growing up, I was a tough kid — tougher than 98 percent of the other kids I knew — and I didn't shy away from trouble. As a result, I got in a lot of fights, usually to defend someone who couldn't defend himself — like little Bobby B., a mentally challenged kid that the other kids would sometimes call "moron" or "retard." Boy, when I heard that, my blood would boil and I would jump in to defend him. I'm still like that. I'm a helpless "jumper-inner." If someone is in trouble or I see a crisis developing, I do something about it. I get my hands dirty. I don't think about it; I just leap before I look. Sometimes that's a good thing, sometimes not.

I'm a natural starter of things.

So when I say "extravert," I don't mean that I love to stand up in front of thousands of people and speak or perform. I just mean I'm outer-directed. My peculiar energies tend to put me out there on the front lines, in interesting and dynamic situations with other people. As a result, I've had more on-the-edge encounters than the average Joe, and this has given me many lifetimes' worth of learning material and "case studies" to draw from.

Think about it. An introvert might meet, say, 1,000 people in his lifetime and, out of those, he will probably have prolonged contact with only a handful.

So his conclusions about his fellow man will be based on a pretty small sample. As for me, best guess is I've probably met 100,000 people in my life, or maybe even twice that number. Of these, I'd say that at least 25,000 encounters have been of sufficient length, breadth, and depth to give me a chance to make some meaningful observations.

It's from those thousands and thousands of encounters that I've been able to distill a few basic truths about human nature, truths that have been papered over by layers of abstract, politically correct thinking in today's education-rich, common sense-poor world. I think these truths were once a lot more obvious to people. Parents taught them to their kids, and people used them to steer a path through the dark forests of life. But somehow, somewhere, we've lost sight of them. Nowadays we spend so much time and energy making a fuss about minor and distracting details — "picking pepper from fly poop," as I like to put it — that we miss some very basic principles of human nature that need to be reexamined. That's what this book is about, the big stuff we forget to look at. I'm probably going to tell you things here that you already know, deep down, but don't think about too often. I'm going to package these ideas in a common-sense, no-nonsense style that both the garbage man and the Harvard grad can get. And believe me, that's no knock on the garbage man! He'll probably see the sense in it immediately; the Harvard grad may have to think about it for a while. But then, I'm not one to knock Harvard grads either.

We'll get into the meat of it all in just a minute, I promise. But first, I want to share just a little bit more about my background and how it led me to write this book.

The Wisdom of the Building Trades

I told you I've been in building construction since I was eight years old. That was no exaggeration. I was in third grade when I starting going to work with my dad on weekends and any other time I wasn't in school, sometimes seven days a week.

I'm the son of a builder and the grandson of builders on both sides of my family. My father was also a master carpenter, so I guess it's no surprise that wood sap flows in my veins. I grew up with a builder's values and ethics: namely, you build good stuff at a fair price, honor your promises, and treat people right.

When I entered the business, we were still part of the "Old World." Things were a lot simpler and more direct. For one thing, you worked with the same guys, on job after job. You had time to get to know them and learn about their philosophies of life and work. You got to acquire some wisdom from them. I can list hundreds of colorful characters I've worked with, shoulder to shoulder, lunch pail to lunch pail. Take Tony the sheet-rocker, who had twelve kids. Every dollar he earned was already spoken for. His only comfort in life was his bottle of cheap vodka, which he drank with uncomplicated enthusiasm. Then there was Eddie, a framer from Canada who enjoyed bar fighting the way some people enjoy fine gourmet chocolates. I remember Bald Eagle, the Micmac Indian tar-and-gravel roofer; Frenchie, the Canadian carpenter who secretly wrote poetry on his pay-stubs; Roy, the Portuguese pipefitter; Alfonzo, the Italian mason... and the list goes on.

There's something about the building trades that gives you a straightforward, unvarnished look at people — and life — that you can't get anywhere else. You learn values that are usable and that teach you how to act.

You see, we builders deal in the "concrete" and observable, not the digital or abstract. You promise a customer you're going to build a wall by Thursday, and then you either deliver on your promise or you don't. There's not much room for bullsh*t. Come Thursday, the wall is either sitting there for all eyes to see and all tools to measure, or it isn't.

Building a house is very different from doing a management consulting job or giving a lecture. It's all about results. Human nature is brought to the forefront. There's no place to hide. If you screw the job up, it's obvious to everyone... and it's your responsibility to fix it.

When I was growing up, guys on the job worked hard. They *had* to. They were all living from week to week. No work meant no food for your family, so everyone gobbled up all the hours they could get, especially the ones with twelve kids to feed.

Construction companies did all their own work, too. That's one of the reasons I had to learn so many trades. Back then, companies didn't subcontract work to other companies. You took responsibility for every nail, rivet, and brick you laid down. If customers had a problem, they knew whom to turn to. Today, it's a different world. Virtually every contractor uses subcontractors for almost all their jobs. Contracting companies have become service brokerages, owned by college graduates who have never picked up a shovel and wouldn't know which end of a hammer drives the nail or which end of the nail to drive. It's hard to know where the buck stops anymore, if it even stops at all. Everyone has someone else they can blame when something goes wrong. Kind of like the phone company or cable company. When you call them with a problem, you know there's not a single human being in that building who can singlehandedly solve it. There's no one to yell at or personally thank anymore; it's all gone mushy. Responsibility is distributed all over the place, and everyone has a way to dodge it. The buck doesn't *stop;* it just runs out of gas and sputters to the side of the road.

But working in the trades, I learned to take 100 percent responsibility for every promise I made — an attribute I've carried into all parts of my life.

Seeing "Behind the Curtain"

Another fascinating thing about the contracting business is that it takes you right into real people's homes, "behind the curtain." It's the ultimate reality show, only without the cameras and the secretly scripted drama. Home contracting provides a sociological study most university researchers would drool over.

When I was a kid, my father and I rebuilt and remodeled kitchens, bathrooms, bedrooms, and family rooms, very intimate stuff. We would show up early in the morning, when most people's guards were down and they were living their lives in a very personal, unpretentious way. We'd get to see them without their makeup on, literally and figuratively. I've done work for people of virtually all cultures and nationalities — Italian, English, Greek, Polish, French, Chinese, Arabic, Jewish, African-American, Indian, Spanish... you name it. They say nothing broadens the mind like travel. Well, being in the *homes* of people of all different cultures, away from the social images they present to the world, is mind broadening like nothing else on Earth. I had the privilege of seeing the way family members of virtually every class and culture interacted, how they prepared for their days, how they expressed love and expectation to each other. I got to see the common threads that weave through people in all cultures, as well as the stuff that's unique.

More than that, I got to observe people under stress. You see, when you're a contractor, people really don't want you in their houses. Even though they hire you to do a job, they do not welcome the actual *doing* of the job. If they could have their way, they would snap their fingers and the job would be instantly finished. The builder's presence in the home is a constant irritant, which stirs the family pot and brings out some revealing behavior.

Contracts and Negotiations

The area of the construction trades where I probably learned the most, though, was in business deals and contracts. The construction business is an endless string of negotiations, contracts, and payments (or nonpayments, as the case may be). I have learned more by watching business deals go down than by observing just about any other human behavior. I can remember, as a young boy, watching the eyes of all the people in a room when my father negotiated a job. Because I was just a kid, I was like an invisible person or part of the furniture, a neutral observer. In absolute fascination, I watched and listened while the deals unfolded. I learned to recognize certain telltale looks in the eye, unconscious pieces of body language, and odd phrases that would tip me off that something was going on below the surface — that one of the parties was up to something.

I also remember seeing the wariness, and *weariness*, on my father's face when a customer tried to con him into providing all sorts of extras at no extra pay. It pained me to see this hardworking, honest man being bled by people who wielded their checkbooks like machetes. Over and over I watched supposedly honest, upright citizens — doctors, judges, teachers, mothers — use the threat of non-payment to persuade my dad to do extra work they knew full well he hadn't agreed to in the first place.

And it wasn't just the customers who cheated at the game. I remember one Italian mason, for instance, who was a true master. During the pre-job negotiations, he always agreed to include a whole list of "extra" services in his base price. His English was flawless (heavily accented, but excellent). *After* the job, he'd itemize those same "extras" and try to charge separately for them. When the customer balked (who could blame them?), the mason would suddenly lapse into "no English" mode, claiming in stumbling half-Italian that he had never agreed to include them. He would play the part of the poor mistreated immigrant, pleading with the customer not to take food out of his children's mouths. The first time I witnessed this, I was practically digging out *my own* wallet to pay him the difference. I soon realized this was just a stunt he pulled on every job.

I would estimate that, over the years, I have been party or witness to at least 10,000 business deals, from a simple window replacement to an entire Greek elderly housing complex. The education I received from watching and listening to these deals go down taught me much of what is in this book and gave me the confidence to start my own business at the tender age of twenty. In a short time, my construction and development business in the Merrimack Valley area of northeast Massachusetts became a major player. Of course, I had to learn things like how to manage money, control expenses, work the permits system, and a thousand other skills, but the skill that has led to the bulk of my success has been my ability to read people.

And what I've learned about people, over all those years and all those deals, boils down to one thing. Ready?

Three Types

There are three types of people. Every single person who walks on this planet falls into one of three basic categories:

A **Taker**

A **Giver,** or...

A **Take-and-Giver** (which I sometimes call a T&G person or a T&Ger)

Figuring out which of these three categories a person (including yourself) falls into is the most important information you will ever need to know when dealing with that person in any kind of relationship. Givers Give, Takers Take, and Take-and-Givers know how to do both. Simplistic? Yes. Overstated? Sure, a bit. But the truth is, human beings become a lot easier to understand, relate to, manage, and do business with, when viewed through this simple lens.

And it's a lens we've forgotten to use in this complicated, media-saturated, politically manipulated world we're now living in. Nowadays, if you call a Taker a Taker, there's always some politician, pundit, or academic waiting in the wings to bite your head off. Political correctness forbids us from speaking the simple truth. But the simple truth is that some people are charged like the negative pole of the battery (Takers), some people are charged like the positive pole (Givers), and some people are able to flip the battery back and forth as the situation requires (T&G people).

If you use the Giver/Taker litmus test with every relationship you're in — family, friends, business, marriage, self, school, neighbors — you will plow through acres of horse crap and gain an enormous leg up on the vast majority of confused and miserable citizens of planet Earth.

And even better, you will gain an enormous leg up on *life*.

Because, as I hope to show in this book, the Give/Take scale affects every single aspect of our lives and every relationship we're in.

Yes, it's simple stuff, but that's why it's useful. I believe the secret to "un-complicating" life is to adopt truthful, simple rules you can keep in your back pocket and use when you need them, like a tape measure. From the time you were a kid, you have remembered not to put your hand on the burner of the stove, right? Why? Because hot stoves hurt you. See? Simple!

This book will simplify what the academics have been complicating and confusing for years. Most academics read about life and theorize about it, but they haven't really lived it. They haven't been street fighters. I have. I've paved the roads of life, literally and figuratively, and I've been fortunate enough not only to survive, but also to prosper, while so many others have not.

I think I've learned a thing or two in the process. All I can do is give you my side of the story…

2

What I Hope You'll Learn

So...

I repeat. People fall into three basic categories: Takers, Givers, and T&Gers.

Again, this is not new or startling information. I don't claim to have discovered the secret to cold fusion or the Unified Field Theory. Moses didn't pull this formula down from the mountaintop on stone tablets (well, maybe he did, a little bit). I don't claim it explains all the joys and complexities of human life or even that it represents some ultimate psychological truth. And for the record, science may never be able to verify it experimentally.

What I *do* claim is that the Give/Take test may be the most important piece of human analysis you can perform on yourself or your fellow man if you want to live richly, happily, successfully, and, most of all, peacefully. Hundreds of millions of human beings have gone to their graves frustrated, unhappy, confused, and bitter because they failed to apply this simple test to one or more of the key relationships in their lives. They were unable to see the Takers who were staring them in the face like hungry hyenas at the watering hole.

On the other hand, the ability to *use* this simple calculus, which I'll flesh out over the course of this short book, has not only given me, personally, a tried-and-true compass for navigating many a sticky social and family situation, but it has also saved me millions of dollars in business mistakes. Over the years I have negotiated hundreds of millions of dollars' worth of business contracts, but I have only lost perhaps a few hundred thousand — a relative drop in the bucket and much less than most guys in my position.

Why? It mainly comes down to one simple step: taking the time and effort to ask myself, "Is this person (or company) a Taker, a Giver, or a Take-and-Giver?" The answer to this question doesn't tell me *every* detail I need to know about the other party, but it gives me my basic approach for dealing with that person, and it rarely steers me wrong.

I may get burned in small ways, but not in big ones.

The fact is, people are "charged" negatively or positively. It's that simple. They really do fit into one of these three categories, and if you don't recognize the important people in your life for what they are, you *will* get hurt and you *will* suffer.

People Are What They Are

I once heard a little story that sort of sums up the situation.

A boy is walking along a riverbank when he spots a crocodile trapped in a net. The croc says to the boy, "Please have pity on me and set me free!"

The boy is touched by the animal's plight, but he's no fool. He says to the croc, "But if I set you free, you'll turn around and eat *me*!"

The croc takes offense. "Do you really think I would do such a thing to my hero and liberator?"

"I *guess* not," says the boy, a tad reluctant. He cuts the croc's head out of the net, and before he can even free the animal's tail, the croc grabs him in its jaws. "This is what I get for my good deed?" cries the boy.

"Don't take it personally," says the croc. "This is just the way of the world, the law of life. Things are what they are."

"I don't believe you!" shouts the boy. "The world can't possibly be so cold and cruel."

"Tell you what," the croc replies. "Because you were so good to me, we'll get a second opinion."

They spot a rabbit running by, call him over, and ask what he thinks of the croc's view of life.

"Did you really say such a thing to the boy?" asks the gentle rabbit in shock.

The croc nods *yes*.

"Well then," says the rabbit, "we need to discuss this."

"Okay," shrugs the croc.

"But how can we have a discussion when you've got a mouthful of boy?" asks the rabbit. "Put him down just for a minute, so we can all take part in the talk."

"Aha! You're a clever one, rabbit," says the croc. "The second I put him down, he'll run away. That's what tasty little boys do."

"But if he tries to do that, you can stop him with a swipe of your mighty tail," says the rabbit.

The croc is persuaded and concedes, but the moment he sets the boy down, the rabbit shouts, "RUN!" and the boy charges off, the rabbit close behind him. Because the croc's tail is still tangled in the net, both the boy and the rabbit manage to escape.

The boy is very grateful to his kind new friend, the rabbit. They walk along for a while together, laughing and chatting. "Wouldn't the villagers love a tasty meal of crocodile meat tonight?" muses the rabbit.

The boy thinks about how great it would feel to be the hero who brings the gift of food to his whole village. "Yes, they would!" he says, and runs home, thanking the kind rabbit one last time.

The villagers take up their weapons and follow the boy back to the river. Without a moment's thought, they kill the crocodile.

The boy's dog, which has tagged along with him, spots the rabbit nearby, gives chase, catches him, and kills him.

As the boy watches his rabbit friend die, he tearfully admits, "The crocodile was right. This is the way of the world and the law of life. Things are what they are."

The point of the story, as you've probably gathered, is that *people* are what they are. In the vast majority of cases, the leopard doesn't change its spots. Crocs are crocs, and rabbits are rabbits. But here's the most important point: Things could have turned out differently for the boy if he had *realized what he was dealing with* and taken the proper precautions.

When we hope for and expect people to deviate from their basic nature, we get hurt. That's where 90 percent of the misery of the world is generated. That's the crucial point I want you to understand.

People are Givers, Takers, or T&Gers, and you need to know which is which.

So Change Isn't Possible?

Does that mean people can't change, that we're all doomed to live out whatever script is encoded in our genes? No. Unlike crocs and rabbits and dogs, animals whose natures are fixed, people *can* change. A young man who kills a clerk while robbing a liquor store *can* — through counseling, self-examination, and a lot of time sitting alone in a prison cell — come to realize the magnitude of what he did and change his ways. A selfish manipulator *can*, with a great deal of effort and commitment, learn to be compassionate. A vindictive person *can* learn forgiveness.

But the thing is, 98 percent of the time, that doesn't happen. Why? Because our basic "charge" — positive or negative — exerts a powerful and steady pull on us, just like the charge of a battery. It's relentless.

Change requires self-awareness, commitment, and willpower, and most people simply don't possess those qualities. *Self-awareness* means being ruthlessly honest with yourself, being willing to look in the mirror at the darkest aspects of your personality and take responsibility for every hurtful choice you have made. *Commitment* means the ability to make a serious promise to change, and *willpower* means having the internal fortitude to keep striving to fulfill that commitment, no matter what.

Most people, most of the time, lack the courage to do any of those things.

So, the sad fact is that 98 percent of the time, people don't change. The guy who beats up his girlfriend, then shows up at her door the next day, bearing flowers and promising he'll never do it again, *will* do it again. The employee who sneaks tools home from the job without asking *will* steal again. The money-borrowing brother-in-law *will* borrow money again. Unless people have some kind of profound, traumatic, life-changing experience, like surviving an airplane crash, or unless they show evidence of *genuine* and *sustained* self-awareness, you can count on crocs being crocs and rabbits being rabbits.

So, you must make your adjustments accordingly. You must change your relationships, protect yourself, and sometimes cut your losses.

Politicians, advertisers, talking heads, media pundits, college professors, and others spend a great deal of time and energy nowadays trying to tell us that Takers aren't really Takers and that Givers aren't really Givers or that the distinctions really aren't that important. But they *are* important — more important than just about anything else in the realm of human intercourse.

It's really pretty easy to spot where a person lies on the Giving/Taking scale, and this book will help you do just that. The difficult part is admitting the truth to yourself and taking action accordingly.

Why I Wrote This Book

So with those preliminary words under our belts, I'd like to explain my main purposes in writing this book. First and foremost, I want to give my family something to pass down, so that future generations will know what their grandfather learned about life. But the three reasons that apply to most readers are:

1. To give you a tool for assessing the relationships in your life. I want to help you figure out where things stand for *you*. In the next chapter, I'll show you the Joe Dial, which I've devised to help you figure out where on the Take-and-Give scale the important people in your life lie. It's a simple visual tool. I believe its usefulness lies in its simplicity. There are many great thinkers out there with important messages for the world, but a lot of what they're selling is just too complicated for our busy, distracted lives. It can't be translated into action. My Joe Dial is simple and clear. I encourage you to *use* it to assess the people who hold important places in your life, in areas such as:

- **Family** — your spouse, your children, your parents, your important relatives
- **Friends and community** — your old friends, new friends, work friends, neighbors
- **Career** — your boss, co-workers, important clients and customers, business partners, suppliers, subcontractors, etc.
- **Leaders** — your elected officials, organizational leaders, spiritual leaders, "thought leaders" (the people you listen to on the radio, watch on TV, or follow in the newspapers)
- **Charity and volunteer work** — the people and organizations to which you offer your time, work, money, and compassion

Know who the Takers and the Givers are in your life, and you won't need to read reams of self-help books, get years of relationship counseling, or put yourself through years of emotional suffering and anguish. You'll know in your gut how to respond. You'll know which relationships are worth investing in, which ones need to change, and which ones need limits set on them. You'll know when to lend support to people and when to pull back on the support you're already Giving.

2. To give you a simple tool to self-analyze. This book will help you ask yourself where YOU lie on the T&G scale. It's a challenging question, but only by answering it honestly will you be able to steer a course toward healthy, productive, and peaceful relationships. If you're too much of a Taker or too much of a Giver, you *will* get hurt and you *will* hurt others, plain and simple. It's time to take stock of where you lie on the scale and decide whether you want to make some changes. Before any of your *relationships* can change, the person doing the relating needs to change... namely, you.

3. To encourage you to change. While it's true that most crocodiles stay crocodiles and that 98 percent of the time people don't change, that's only part of the story. The other part is that some people DO change; in fact, *all* of the great ones do. While you should never, ever fall into the trap of *expecting others to change* (since that's just not something you can control or predict), you can and should expect yourself to change. In fact, you should *demand* it.

But you can't change without knowing where you are right now.

It's all about *awareness*, my friend. It's about recognizing the basic energy charge you're currently carrying. You can't change as long as you continue to deny, distort, ignore, or rationalize your true Give/Take nature. You must fully accept your basic charge, your basic orientation toward life, your basic spin. Only then do you have the freedom to change.

Ninety-five percent of our prison cells are populated by people who see themselves as victims of circumstance, who rationalize their behavior, who minimize or deny what they did, or who blame others for their bad decisions and dream only of revenge. But every once in a while, one of those prisoners sits up, looks at himself in the steel mirror, and says, "Oh my God! What have I done?" and that's the exact moment the process of change can begin. Change is hard, but it's absolutely impossible without self-awareness and awareness of the basic nature of your relationships.

Most people *don't* change, BUT…

People *can* change and people *do* change.

And I believe, by the fact that you are reading this book, you are one of those people. My hope is that this book will help you take a step toward greater awareness so that you can be one of those rare souls who *does* change and in so doing inspires those around you to do the same.

There are too many Takers in today's world, but we cannot change that by force, manipulation, or legislation. We can change that only by our own willingness to change ourselves, and when we do this, we gently encourage others to do the same.

3

The Joe Dial

Every now and then, an experience in life can crystallize a vague concept that's floating around in your mind and smack you in the head like a two-by-four. I recall one particular experience that really gelled the ideas in this book for me and brought them into sharp focus.

About twenty years ago, one of our local newspapers was running an annual charity called Santa's Fund. The way it worked was that people wrote in to the paper to share their stories of personal hardship, basically making a case as to why they deserved a little help during the holiday season. It was a well-intentioned charity that certainly had its heart in the right place, and some of the stories that came in were heartbreaking.

I was reading some of these stories with my wife, and…

Well, as I said, I'm an incurable jumper-inner. When I see a problem that needs solving, I'm pretty quick to get up off the couch and try to do something about it. So that particular Christmas season, feeling blessed as I was by my own good fortune and feeling the tug of the Christmas spirit, I decided to help — only I wanted to do it *my* way, 'cause that's the way I roll. I opted to cut out the middleman — namely Santa's Fund itself — and make my holiday contribution directly to the parties who needed it. A couple of friends of mine who had also had some financial success agreed to join me. The three of us decided to pony up several thousand dollars of our own money and play Santa. We decided to take our kids along, too, to show them how lucky they were and to include them in the holiday Giving.

We rallied our work trucks together and loaded them up with turkeys, Christmas dinners, goodies, clothing, and gifts for kids — a nice blend of necessities and holiday extras. Using the list of names we got from Santa's Fund, we started making the holiday rounds in person, taking our Christmas cheer directly to the people who needed it most.

As it turned out, though, I was the one who got the Christmas surprise. The majority of the people my friends and I visited had no true need for the stuff we were Giving out. I'm not saying their homes were *palaces* — they weren't — but many of them had big TVs, Nintendos, and most of the gadgets that every middle-class home has, including heat, hot water, electricity, and recent-model cars in the driveways. The kids had decent clothes and new sneakers.

In short, these were not people who needed me to be Giving them *stuff*.

My friends and I felt like idiots, embarrassed and duped. We were a little ticked off, too, frankly. What were we teaching our children?

Now, of course, some of the recipients *did* need the stuff and would not have had a holiday celebration without it, but the truly needy people were in the minority. That fact was sadly obvious.

I realize this story may rub some of you the wrong way. There's been a tendency on the part of some media folks to tell tall tales about welfare mothers buying lobster and Dom Pérignon with food stamps and driving BMWs to the welfare office. Many of these stories are undoubtedly made up, *but* there's been just as large a tendency among others to dismiss all of these stories as pure urban myth. All I can tell you is what I saw with my own eyes. (As I told you, I like to put myself out there on the front lines of experience.) Many of the people for whom we were trying to do a charitable act were, in fact, inveterate Takers. These were not truly needy people; these were people used to living on the system and relying on others to provide for them.

What I Learned

A simple truth was staring me in the face: Takers Take what Givers Give. It's their nature. It's not that most Takers are evil or ill intentioned, but put some motivated Takers in the company of some motivated Givers, and the Givers will quickly end up with much less of their stuff. It's really that simple. Takers create a vacuum, and Givers fill it. (And when we make it easy, shameless, and painless for the Takers to Take, as we do through government giveaway programs, we turn Taking into an institution that creates more Takers. We'll talk about that more, later in the book.)

This Santa story does have a happy ending though. My partners and I finally called a halt to our ho-ho-ho activities and went to the local church for help. The church was able to furnish us with a list of folks who *really did* need our help. Interestingly enough, these people weren't the ones advertising in the paper with their hard-luck stories. They were much quieter, humbler, and more reluctant about it. Yes, they needed help, but they weren't comfortable coming out and asking for it. Why? Because they weren't seasoned, professional Takers.

I had to ask myself, "If Takers are shameless enough to hijack the holiday compassion of their fellow man and use *Santa Claus* as a tool for extracting more stuff from Givers, what else might they be willing to do?" God only knows.

I realized, after this experience, that the time had come to strip away the stories we tell ourselves about our fellow man and to look at this thing on a purely elemental, energetic level. *Taking*-energy is a powerful force that pulls things to it, like a magnet. Taking-energy can come in a thousand forms — a boss who only wants production out of his workers without paying them fairly, a healthy young man or woman who would rather collect government checks than work, a guy who only wants sex from his wife or girlfriend. We can obscure the truth about Takers and Givers with politically correct words and concepts, but unless we look at what's really going on, energetically speaking, we'll never get our private lives or our political systems in order.

The Joe Dial

That said, I'm going to present you with the simple visual model I use to assess my fellow man — and myself — from time to time.

THREE KINDS OF PEOPLE

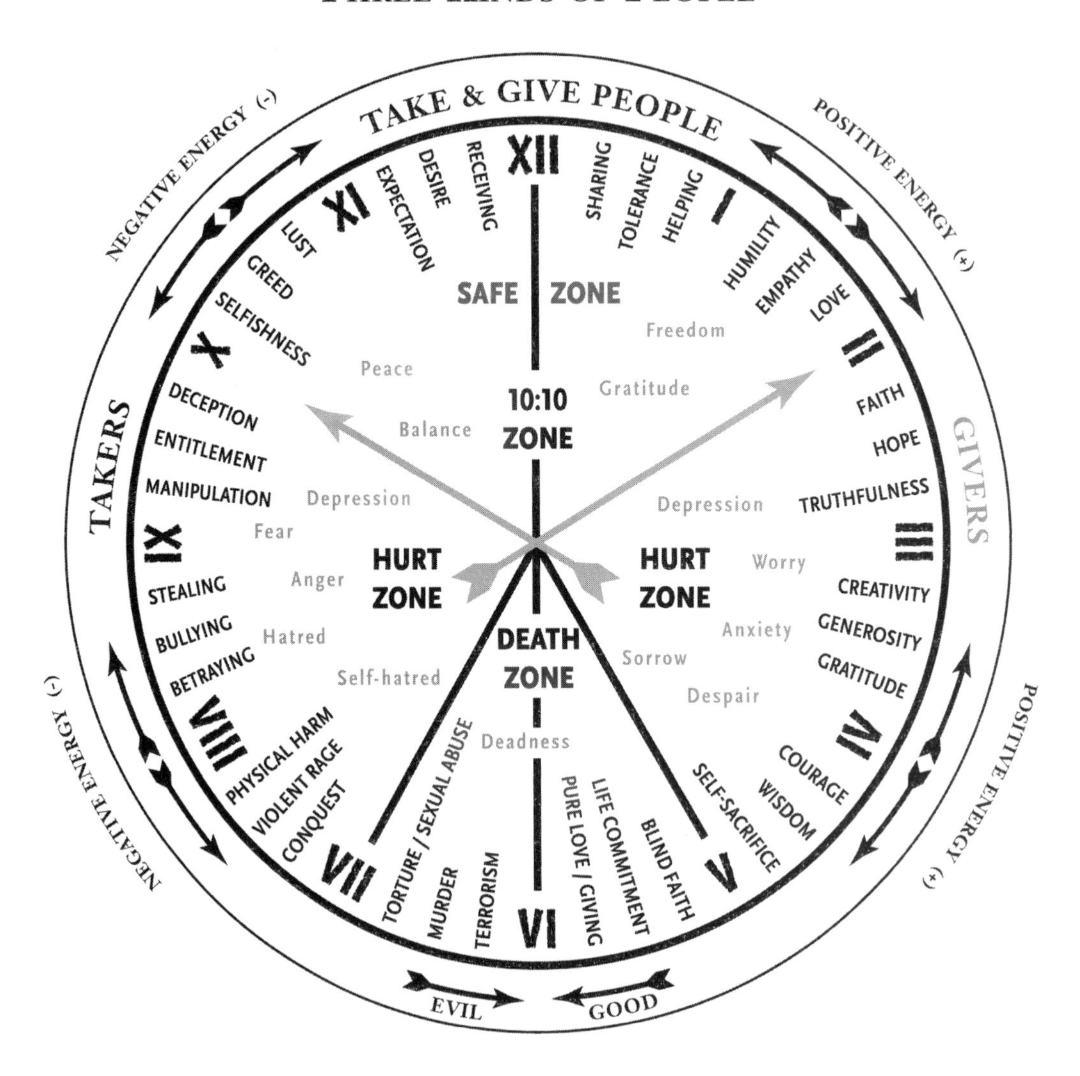

As you've surely figured out by now, I call it the Joe Dial, though it also contains characteristics of a compass, a clock, and a medallion. It's like a *compass* because it shows a person's basic magnetic "pull" and because we can use it as a guide. It's like a *clock* because it uses the twelve clock numbers as handy references and clock hands to mark movement. It's like a *dial* because you can move the hands manually — that is, you can *choose* to work on becoming more of a Giver or more of a Taker (yes, there are reasons to become more of a Taker, which we'll get into shortly). Finally, it's like a *medallion* because you can "hang" it on people to visually represent where they fall on the Give/Take scale. But let's call it a Dial for the sake of convenience.

You may notice a familiar shape embedded in the Joe Dial. It's the peace symbol. Why is that there? Because I believe the only way to attain peace within yourself and within your relationships is by finding the balance between Taking and Giving. Peace, in fact, is the real purpose for using the Dial.

So let's look at what the Dial shows us.

THE "GIVE" SIDE

The right-hand side of the Dial, from twelve to six, as you can see, is the Giving side, the side of Good. All positive emotions and tendencies fall on this side of the Dial. It is the home of the seven great virtues (my list differs from the traditional Christian seven):

Truth
Love
Courage
Creativity
Tolerance
Freedom
Wisdom

The Giving side of the Dial spans the range of human qualities from sharing, tolerance, and helping; through empathy, love, and truthfulness; through generosity and gratitude; all the way to the final point, which we can call "pure love and Giving." This final sliver of the Dial, from about minute twenty-nine to minute thirty, is one in which only a few rare human beings ever dwell. It is the land of true saints, enlightened beings who are capable of Giving and loving without needing anything in return. When it comes to true saints, all the rules I talk about in this book break down. But that's okay, because if you ever find yourself living in that zone, you won't be buying self-help books anymore. (*I'll* be buying books from you!) The problem is, some people try to force themselves to emulate saints — fighting the Good fight, 24/7 — when they're not spiritually equipped for the job, and they pay a huge price for it. We'll get into that soon.

THE "TAKE" SIDE

The left-hand side of the Dial, from six to twelve, is the Taking side. Not to be confused with *political* leftness, this is the dark side, the negative side, and, toward the bottom, the home of true evil. Not all of the Taking zone is evil, but all of it does represent a "me" orientation — *my* needs, *my* desires, *my* goals. It is the land of the Seven Deadly Sins:

Pride
Envy
Greed
Sloth
Gluttony
Lust
Anger

It spans from simple receiving and desire; through greed, deception, outright stealing, and betrayal; through physical harming and rage; and into the truly dark realms. As on the opposite side of the Dial, there are only a few people who dwell in the last few ticks between six and seven. People who live in this zone are the violent rapists, serial killers, and pedophiles all of society would categorize as evil. These people operate by their own rules and are probably immune to any insight a book like this might offer. They have sunk so deep in Taking that there is little or no hope for change.

How the Population Breaks Down

Again, people fall into three basic categories, but those categories are on a continuum. I estimate the rough percentages as:

Givers — 15% of the population

Takers — 15% of the population

Take-and-Givers (T&G people) — 70% of the population

About 15 percent of us are Givers who spend the vast majority of our time on the right side of the Dial. We might dip into the Taking side during moments of crisis or when our safety and livelihood is threatened, but we quickly spring back. For example, Jesus Christ himself is known to have lost His cool on the moneylenders and merchants when He saw them plying their trade outside a temple. His needle shot into the violent range of the Taking side at that moment, but then it quickly reset itself on the Giving side.

About 15 percent of us are Takers who spend the vast majority of our time on the Taking side of the Dial. We might have the occasional charitable impulse, but it's only a flash in the pan. We immediately revert to our comfort zone, namely, watching out for old Number One. Famed serial killer, torturer, and cannibal Jeffery Dahmer, for example, was known to move his neighbors' trash barrels back into their yards as a courtesy and to help the proverbial old lady cross the street. But those impulses, we can only assume, were momentary spikes of the compass needle. His needle quickly resettled in the darker regions.

About 70 percent of us are T&Gers, Take-and-Givers. We don't live entirely on either side of the Dial, and we often flip back and forth. And that's a good thing, for the most part, though not always. Some people flip to *extreme* points on the Dial with apparent randomness, according to unseen whims of their psyches or their biochemistry. Such people are mentally/emotionally unstable and potentially dangerous. They are unpredictable and difficult to be in any kind of relationship with. The most dangerous psychopaths often have that quality of unpredictability. They may act sweet and generous one moment and flare into a rage the next. It's actually easier to relate to a pure Taker than a Random Extreme Flipper. These people put everyone in a constant state of anxiety.

But those of us who are able to flip back and forth within a limited "safety" range of Taking and Giving are the most mentally/emotionally healthy people. I refer to this safety range as the **10:10 Zone**.

The 10:10 Zone and the Hurt Zone

The 10:10 Zone is so named because it's defined by the two hands of the clock when the time is 10:10. I also like the term 10:10 because it conveys a nice sense of balance.

And that's what the 10:10 Zone is all about: balance. Those of us who live mostly within the 10:10 Zone — even if we occasionally spike into the other zones — are stable, reasonable, and fairly well balanced. We know how to Give *and* Take, both of which are extremely important for a peaceful life.

It is highly desirable to be in relationships with people whose Dial needles stay largely within the 10:10 Zone. I will make that point repeatedly throughout this book. The 10:10 Zone is where we want to strive to live.

The Hurt Zones are the areas we want to avoid, at least as permanent residences. We can *visit* them, but we don't want to park our cars there. The Hurt Zones are those large zones on the southerly part of either side of the Dial. They represent the more extreme ends of the Give and Take spectrum. People who dwell *primarily* in either of these zones hurt themselves and/or others. They live in an out-of-balance way, due to a shortage of either Giving or Taking energy.

You might think that only the extreme Takers would fall prey to Hurt, but that's not the case. Extreme Givers are just as vulnerable to Hurt as Takers. Not only are they Taken by Takers, but they typically find themselves in trouble with their health, their finances, their careers, their families, and their relationships. While it's great to spend some time in the high numbers of the Giving side, it's important not to get stuck there.

We'll see why as we delve into the three types a little more deeply…

4

Givers and Takers

Most of us fall somewhere in the T&G range, a mix of Taker and Giver, but there are many pure Givers and Takers among us too. The Dial needles of these folks rest fairly permanently on either the Taking side or the Giving side. Again, each of these groups accounts for only about 10 or 15 percent of the population, but that is still a substantial minority.

Givers

There are both positive and negative aspects to being a Giver. Let's take a quick look at both.

THE PROS

A Giver is a sincere, honest person with a driving sense of concern for the world and everyone in it. Givers feel a responsibility to treat everyone with dignity and respect. They see it as their duty to leave the world in better shape than they find it. They hate injustice and have a tendency to take the wrongs of society personally. They have a positive orientation toward every situation and are always concerned with what they are bringing to the table rather than what they are Taking from it. They are always willing to contribute more than their share —

financially, physically, and emotionally. They care about the people around them in every situation and want to make others comfortable and happy.

Givers have strong values that direct most of the decisions they make in life. They typically eat healthy food, work out to stay fit, try to get enough sleep, and avoid dangerous substances. They care about the environment and make day-to-day decisions that reflect this sense of caring. They recycle, they conserve, they drive fuel-efficient vehicles. They even drink fair-trade coffee.

Many Givers are religious and attend church or temple regularly. They tend to see themselves as part of a bigger picture and to see their lives as meaningful. They Give money to charity and volunteer their time for charity efforts, putting their money and their action where their mouths are.

They also care about their families and try to spend time with them. They try to make sure their children are exposed to good ideas. They may even send them to private schools, at great sacrifice and expense, just to be sure they are learning healthy values. They are financially generous with friends and family members. Your burden is their burden.

As employees, Givers are tirelessly dedicated. As employers, they are generous, trusting, and flexible. They try to make everyone on their team happy, and they cut people a lot of slack when they fall short of expectations. They prefer to seal a deal with a handshake rather than a pile of contracts. When other people do them wrong, they see them as misguided, misinformed, or in need of help, rather than as Takers.

THE CONS

There's a dark side to Giving, however.

The danger for people who live *only* in the Giving Zone is that they can be easily taken advantage of by Takers. The pure Giver often fails to assess a situation to make sure his/her interests are being protected. S/he tends to be extremely trusting and to assume that everyone has the best of intentions. Because Givers use themselves as a reference point, they assume others would not knowingly harm or cheat them. They truly don't understand the Taking mentality, so they do not realize there is a whole class of people out there, eager to Take everything they are willing to Give and then some.

Givers tend to blame themselves when someone harms them, and although taking responsibility for one's own behavior is an admirable trait, *too much* self-blame can blind Givers to the evil crap other people are trying to pull on them. Relentless Givers tend to compromise their health, their happiness, and their peace of mind. In their endless zeal to save the world, they often fail to save themselves.

A Giver with no Take in him/her is truly in danger of losing everything to a clever Taker. We read all the time about innocent folks losing their life savings through misguided trust in a conman. And the really terrible thing is that Givers can become hopelessly disillusioned when their trust is ruptured in this way. They can plunge into despair and negativity or, even worse, they can blindly revert to their old ways, setting themselves up for another disaster.

Many people who are incapable of Taking (receiving) turn out to have deep issues of poor self-worth. In some dark place inside them, they don't think they *deserve* to receive anything. They believe their only worth in life comes from constantly making others happy.

One of the most insidious aspects of an all-Give orientation is that it interrupts the natural flow of Give and Take in relationships. Essentially, pure Givers inadvertently stunt the Giving impulses of everyone around them because they don't know how to Take and they don't allow others to Give to them. That leaves the other party in the relationship with no healthy way to exercise *their own* Giving impulses. This is an unfair thing to do to another person. Constant Givers basically turn their partners into Takers. How? Well, when the partner realizes the Giver can only operate in Giving mode, the partner lapses into habitual Taking mode, because it's the only way to relate to the Giver.

Then, after years of all Give and no get, the Giver often becomes angry, resentful, or depressed.

Parents who are all Give, with no expectations of reciprocity, raise children who don't know how to do anything but Take. Societies that Give without demanding anything in return create classes of citizens who are hardened Takers. They interrupt the basic law of survival of the fittest and create a new law: survival of the nonproductive.

I do want to point out that there is also, as I suggested earlier, a unique category of Giver whose consciousness goes beyond the normal limits. These are the Super-Givers, the true saints among us. Mother Theresa was an example of this. Another is Mata Amritanandamayi, otherwise known as the Hugging Saint. Saints — and I don't use the term with sarcasm or irony — are those who have reached a level where they no longer seem to have any need to Take at all. They have become true servants of humanity. They are the purest of the pure Givers and live in a place where the normal rules no longer apply. They seem to channel Universal Love in undiluted form.

But it's important to realize that these are very, very rare souls. Those of us who try to *act* like saints without having attained the enlightened consciousness of saints pay an enormous price in terms of our health, relationships, life expectancy, and sanity.

For most of us, we *must* balance our Giving nature with at least *some* Taking. Giving is a great place to spend *much*, albeit not *all*, of our time and energy.

Takers

Now let's move to the Taking side of the Dial.

Let's be clear on one thing, right up front: Taking, in and of itself, is not a bad thing. Again, we all must have a bit of Taker in us, if only to afford others opportunities to be Givers. Takers are not necessarily bad people. In many cases, they have simply been raised to be Takers by having been Given too much, either by indulgent parents or by society itself. A fourth-generation welfare recipient, for example, has been given no model *but* Taking. Taking is, in a very real sense, his/her family profession. The same might be said for many second- or third-generation trust fund babies.

Taking-energy is negative. Negative doesn't mean *bad*; it just means negative. The negative pole of the car battery is not evil; it merely offers a different charge from the positive pole. It *draws in* energy, while the positive pole *puts out* energy. Both are needed in order for electricity to flow.

Evil only enters the picture when we move far left of the twelve mark on the Dial and fail to balance our Taking with Giving.

THE CONS

Pure Takers are at the opposite end of the human spectrum from pure Givers. They are motivated almost purely by self-interest. Their entire orientation in life is one of receiving, of trying to maximize the gain, rather than the Give, in every situation. A true Taker operates out of a position of fear, always assuming there won't be enough to go around, always strategizing so he gets his share and more.

There are active Takers and passive Takers. *Active Takers* go out and grab whatever they feel entitled to. *Passive Takers* simply open up a gaping vacuum of need that the Givers around them feel compelled to fill.

The Taker, like the Giver, has only himself as a reference point, so he assumes the rest of the world is as Taking-oriented as he is. He believes everyone he deals with, in life and in business, is trying to maximize his or her own advantage. The Taker thinks everyone is out to get him. For the active Taker, this often translates into a "best defense is a good offense" strategy. The active Taker goes after what he wants, stomping on the rights and concerns of others in the process. Seeing the universe as a dog-eat-dog arena, the Taker plays by his own rules, which he rewrites at his own convenience. He will revert to platitudes like "Business is business" to justify all kinds of nasty, unethical behavior.

Passive Takers believe the world owes them a better life than the one they are currently living. No matter where they lie on the economic scale, they are jealous of others who have more than they do. Complaining is their mode of life. Resentment, bitterness, and envy are their common emotions. Neediness is their operating principle. While an *active* Taker will target both Takers and Givers as victims, the *passive* Taker just turns up the need and waits for Givers to provide.

Aggression is part of the active Taker's arsenal — bullying, intimidating, abusing, threatening, and even using physical and/or financial force if they deem it necessary. The passive Taker uses passive-aggressive behavior. When others expect him to live up to his responsibilities and share in the Giving, he resorts to moodiness, resistance, procrastination, or deliberately doing a poor job. He is often late, unreliable, sulky, and hard to pin down. So-called "learned helplessness" is part of his bag of tricks. Because he does not see himself as a contributor, he always expects to be relieved of his duties as quickly as possible and resume his Taking posture. If the old Volkswagen commercials were right that "On the road of life, there are passengers and there are drivers," the passive Taker is always a passenger... and the street *all* Takers ride on is a one-way street that leads to ME.

Honesty is not a high priority for any Taker, unless it happens to serve his/her purposes. If honesty is going to cost him anything, he cheerfully abandons it. The Taker considers it okay to take advantage of others, as this is seen as just part of the game. Takers will lie, cheat, and mislead to get what they want. They will rewrite every scene in life so that it plays to their own advantage. Takers will steal credit for the work of others.

Because Takers are dominated by receiving-energy, rather than producing-energy, they tend to be *consumers*. Their lives often revolve around filling an endless cycle of needs. They may eat too much, drink too much, sleep too much, and have out-of-proportion sexual appetites. They are highly vulnerable to addiction for a couple of reasons. First, their Taking-energy is never satisfied. (They think, "If one drink or one cupcake is good, then *seven* must be better!") Second, they often resort to anaesthetizing themselves to escape the guilt and pain that result from the shabby way they treat others.

The perennial Taker, like the perennial Giver, interrupts the natural Give-and-Take of life by always standing on the Taking side. By doing this, the Taker not only cheats others, but also robs himself. How? He does not allow himself to experience the joy of unselfish Giving, which truly is the highest joy in life. Next to the joy of Giving, the joy of getting pales by comparison. But only those of us who are able to Give — at least some of the time — learn this valuable truth. While it certainly feels good to receive, *constant* receiving becomes an empty, hollow exercise that never offers true fulfillment.

The pure Taker is to be pitied because he never discovers the joy that goes beyond the material and superficial. His life is an endless, hopeless quest for fulfillment through power, prestige, position, and *stuff*.

THE PROS

Taking does play a very vital role in life, though. We all need to wear the Taking hat from time to time to make sure we're protecting our interests from extreme Takers. If we can't look at the world from a Taking point of view, at least part of the time, we *will* get hurt.

Being able to fluidly shift into Taking mode is essential for any kind of healthy relationship: employer/employee, husband/wife, parent/child, friends, business partners, or team members. As mentioned before, without being able to Take, we interrupt the flow of Giving from others and force them to stay in Taking mode.

Are you starting to see how this works? If we never Take, we handicap the Givers in our lives; we provide nowhere for their Giving-energy to go.

Again, it's a matter of energy exchange. A positive charge needs to meet a negative charge, or it cannot flow. That's simple electromagnetism. Two positive charges repel each other, just like when you try to put two batteries together at the + ends or like those little black-and-white magnetic dog toys they used to sell when I was a kid.

Seen from this perspective, Taking is a way of encouraging and promoting Giving. Being a total non-Taker is just as irresponsible as being a total non-Giver. Taking includes accepting, receiving, and welcoming, all of which are important. Taking generates gratitude, which is one of the greatest and most healing emotions mankind can experience. A life without Taking is a life without gratitude or appreciation — a poor life for sure.

To Take, in a healthy way, means to be able to:

- Accept a compliment
- Let someone else buy dinner
- Accept credit when you deserve it
- Sincerely say "Thank you" and "You're welcome"
- Allow someone else to do you a kindness
- Say "I need you" to another person
- Ask for help
- Accept a gift without feeling an immediate need to return the favor
- Speak up for your fair share
- Point out when someone else is trying to take advantage of you
- Reap the harvest of your hard work and goodwill

There must be Give and Take in all good relationships. Too much or too little of either, and you interrupt the natural flow of energy.

And this brings us to the third category of human being...

5

The T&G Person

Equidistant from the pure Taker and the pure Giver on the Dial is the group of us that represents a mix of both Taker and Giver.

The Take-and-Giver — Life in the 10:10 Zone

The T&Ger strikes a balance between Taking and Giving. S/he lives in the 10:10 Zone of the Dial. The T&Ger has developed a working set of instincts about when to Give and when to Take. As a general rule, a T&G person wants neither to take advantage of others nor be taken advantage of. S/he both extends courtesy and expects courtesy in return. S/he understands the concept of true sharing.

T&Gers are evident by some of these common signs:

- They let *you* pay for lunch one day but insist upon paying the next time.
- They are able to both lend a hand and ask for help.
- They listen and talk in roughly equal measure.
- They carry their weight on a team but don't allow themselves to be used.
- They're not excessive with either lending or borrowing.

- They generally work hard but also expect to be fairly compensated.
- They share the driving, the expenses, the workload, and the responsibilities with friends and family members.
- They clean up their own messes, literally and figuratively.
- They may slip into Taking mode from time to time, but they snap out of it before long.
- They may slip into the higher Giving mode from time to time, too, but they are not in danger of getting carried away on a "spiritual high" and losing all good judgment and common sense (as Givers who *dwell* in the Hurt Zone can often do).

Sixty to seventy percent of us fall somewhere within the spectrum of T&Gers. Again, Take-and-Givers are the people with whom you can safely be in a relationship — work relationship, family relationship, love relationship, friendship relationship, or business relationship. You can trust them — not always and not absolutely, but as a general rule — because they are capable of seeing situations from both the Giving and Taking angle. They are not always gunning for self-advantage, as Takers are, nor are they blind to deceit and con games as Givers often are. They are not likely to Give away the store in a business deal, nor are they likely to make unreasonable demands. They are capable of compromise and of looking at the big picture for all parties.

Take-and-Givers can safely have relationships with both Givers *and* Takers. They have the street smarts to spot a Taker and to put sufficient safeguards in place to protect themselves from harm. They prefer the company of Givers, of course, and may sometimes help a Giver avoid being taken advantage of by a Taker. T&Gers can often help Givers find more balance.

The Journey Toward Balance and Wholeness

The goal of healthy human beings is to strike a comfortable balance between Giving and Taking. Each of us starts out with a particular genetic predisposition toward being a Taker, a Giver, or a T&Ger. I believe this is coded into our DNA. It's not that we're *pre-determined*, but we definitely have built-in tendencies, just as we have tendencies toward certain skills, talents, weaknesses, and personality traits. We'll talk about this in an upcoming chapter.

We are also raised by our parents in a way that either encourages Taking or Giving (or both). This contributes greatly to where we end up on the Dial. Our parents cannot change the basic personality traits that are encoded into us, just as a farmer can't change a tomato seedling into a carrot plant, but they *can* nourish certain traits and starve others. They can provide us with good emotional nutrients or rob us of the same, just as the farmer can grow healthy, red tomatoes or stunted, diseased ones. We'll talk about *this* in a later chapter, too.

But here's the point I want to make right now: No matter where we end up on the T&G scale, we *all* start out with our lives weighted heavily toward the Taking end. That's just the way human beings are made. Unlike other animals that are self-sufficient shortly after they're born, humans must rely on their parents for many years. That means, in the early years, we are all Take, Take, Take. We count on our mothers to Give, Give, Give (and we develop many of our basic attitudes about Giving and Taking based on how well Mom plays her role. We'll talk about this later, too.)

We are little Takers, all of us — and that's how it should be — but we are designed to gradually shift *away* from being Taking-dominated to Giving-dominated as we mature. Ideally, by the time we embark on parenthood, we should have shifted our emphasis heavily toward the Giving side of the Dial.

Becoming more Giving does not just allow us to be better parents and citizens, it allows us to reach whole new levels of happiness and fulfillment. The more we practice Giving, the more we learn the subtle rewards that come from the Giving side of the Dial, such as:

- The joy of making another person happy
- The peace of mind that comes from treating others right
- The satisfaction of being a good citizen, team member, or family member

- The relief of letting go of self-protection, greed, and self-interest
- The feeling of freedom that honesty brings
- The beauty of the Giving paradox — that the more we Give, the more good things seem to circle back to us
- "Spiritual" satisfaction

The joy of Giving is an acquired taste, however, compared to the in-your-face "joy" of Taking a cookie from another kid or moving a pile of cash from someone else's bank account into your own. Maturity is required to appreciate the subtle rewards of Giving. A lot of folks, unfortunately, become arrested in their development. For a variety of reasons, they become unable to move out of a Taking mentality and "graduate" into Giving. They become dominated by fear and mistrust. Show me a hardened Taker and I'll show you someone who is emotionally undeveloped and fear-driven.

Others, however, become addicted to the approval they get from Giving. Because they lack a basic feeling of self-worth, they think the only way others will value them is if they are constantly providing something of value, such as sex, work, favors, money, caretaking, praise, or all of the above. Show me a hardened Giver and I'll show you someone who feels fundamentally unworthy.

But again, the normal course of healthy growth is supposed to lead us from being predominantly Takers to being dwellers in the 10:10 Zone, where we can both Give and Take, at least some of the time.

It is crucial to identify the Givers, the Takers, and the T&G people in all of your life relationships. Embrace the T&Gers; beware of the others.

Only Time Tells

It often takes time to figure out whether someone is truly a T&Ger. That's because a person may *appear* to be either a pure Giver or a pure Taker if they happen to be in either of these modes when we meet them for the first time.

Imagine sitting in a conference room, waiting for a meeting to start, and the featured speaker walks in the door, laughing with his colleagues and patting them on the back. He then turns to the room and tells a joke that cracks everyone up. You immediately feel light and at ease. Why? Because you assume you are in the presence of a Giver.

Imagine the opposite. You're waiting for the meeting to start, and the featured speaker walks in, embroiled in an argument. His face is red with rage. He barks a command at one of his team members, then immediately lodges a complaint about the coffee or the projector equipment. How do you feel? Tense and uncomfortable. Why? You assume a Taker has entered the room.

At the moment, you are right in both cases. You are in the presence of Giving-energy in the first case and Taking-energy in the latter, but neither of these assumptions may turn out to be true in the long run. It may be that the apparent Giver is just in a rare great mood or that he turns on the charm whenever he's about to do a presentation. It may also be that the apparent Taker is just having a bad day. Perhaps the airline lost his luggage, or he just found out his wife is having an affair, and now he has to do this stupid presentation.

In most cases, only time reveals whether the people in our lives have their needles stuck on the Giving side or the Taking side of the Dial or whether they live in the 10:10 Zone. Of course, if we see someone rob a liquor store, we can pretty much assume we're looking at a Taker. But for the most part, it's important not to make a snap judgment about this.

The journey toward being a T&Ger is not always smooth and direct. Many of us — most of us, actually — grow in fits and starts and learn our lessons at the great University of Hard Knocks. For example, we may need to go through a painful divorce in order to learn the importance of Giving, or we may need to watch our life's work get stolen by a co-worker in order to learn how to be *less* Giving and more self-protective.

All of us approach the journey toward wholeness from different angles. If you have been a doormat all of your life, it may be important for you to go through a period of intense Taking in order to learn more about that side of the Dial. Someone who meets you during this time might incorrectly assume you are a true Taker. They would be wrong, however. You are simply trying to correct an imbalance in your life. Similarly, if you have always been too much of a Taker in your relationships, you might need to go through a period of intense Giving, such as a stint in the Peace Corps or a spiritual retreat, to find new balance.

What does this mean? We need to look at the *whole context* of a person's life to know whether they are true Takers, true Givers, or simply T&Gers in progress.

The real keys, once again, are *awareness* and *commitment to change*. Does the person have the self-awareness to see the imbalance in his/her life and the commitment and willpower to do something about it? If so, then there's good reason for hope. If not, then the crocodile will remain a crocodile, the dog a dog, and the rabbit a rabbit.

The Peace Place of the 10:10 Zone (the Ideal Person)

Again, the people with whom we want to be in relationships are T&G people, people who live in the 10:10 Zone, and that's where we ourselves want to live. In fact, you'll never survive as an honest and respected businessperson, friend, or family member if you stray out of the 10:10 Zone long term. But there's a little more to the story, and I'd like to refine this idea a bit.

The fact is, there's still quite a bit of range, even within the 10:10 Zone. Just because someone is *tolerable* to work with or hang out with or date doesn't necessarily mean they're *desirable*. While it is possible to have safe, sound dealings with almost anyone who stays within the 10:10 Zone, that doesn't necessarily mean we'll be *happy* with that person.

For example, the person who lives right around the number ten, but who *occasionally* moves over to the Giving side to offer care and encouragement, is still going to be a challenge to work with and live with. His Dial needle is at home in the negative. He's the type that might typically be described by others as "a bit of a jerk," "kind of an a**hole," or "pretty full of himself." He does not cross the line into being an outright manipulator, thief, or abuser, but he will be "high maintenance." He's not someone whose company you'll really enjoy or with whom you'll want to share a truly intimate or trusting relationship.

The people we *really* enjoy — the ones we're *really* drawn to, the ones with whom we can have not only a *workable* relationship, but also a happy and rewarding one — live in what I call the Peace Place. Folks who live in the Peace Place:

- Have Dial needles that tend to hover near two o'clock
- Spend 60 to 70 percent of their time and energy in Giving mode
- Spend only 30 to 40 percent of their time and energy in Taking mode
- Often spike into the higher Giving Zones, all the way to five and six o'clock on the Dial, but remain grounded enough to return to about a two o'clock as an everyday resting place
- Almost never stray south of the number ten on the Taking side of the Dial; if they do, it's a temporary blip (like Mother Theresa kicking a cat), and they quickly recalibrate back to one or two o'clock

People who dwell in the Peace Place of the 10:10 Zone make ideal business and relationship partners. These folks are generally more concerned with Giving than Taking, but they are worldly-wise enough not to be abused or taken advantage of. They can relax and enjoy being treated well — even pampered from time to time — and are more than happy to return the favor. Their basic orientation is, "What can I bring to the table?" but they are not obsessive or compulsive about Giving. They do it in a relaxed, natural way. They also love to receive when the time is right. They are grateful and appreciative. They accept and Give rewards with equal grace and responsibility.

Their Giving is not based in a feeling of unworthiness, but in a positive belief that *contributing* to all relationships and to society as a whole feels good and that it truly is better to Give than to receive. This person views his purpose in life as one of *adding value* to the world, not just acquiring toys, privilege, power, and status.

A person living in the Peace Place does not approach relationships out of a sense of neediness, but rather out of a sense of cooperation, sharing, and mutual growth and support. The often-quoted line from *Jerry Maguire*, "You complete me," would nauseate this person. She knows it is her own responsibility to complete *herself* and that two people can only have a healthy relationship when it is based on positive sharing between two whole and healthy adults.

We'll talk later in the book about some simple ways to steer ourselves toward living in the Peace Place, but for now, we're going to look at some additional factors that will help us use the Dial more accurately. Then we're going to step back and look at how the whole Give-and-Take dynamic got started in the first place and how we keep the cycle going in our own families. A little Nature, a little Nurture, and a little History According to Joe.

Let's roll on...

6

3 + 3 + 3
Three Kinds of People, Three Intelligence Levels, Three Energy Levels

I want to emphasize again that this book does not claim that *every* aspect of human life comes down to where people stand on the Dial or that using the Dial can solve every problem. Life is full of richness and subtlety. My point in writing this book is to say that if we get so caught up in the subtlety that we miss the big stuff, we're picking pepper out of fly poop again.

Think of it this way:

Many interesting events were happening on the *Titanic* on that fateful evening in 1912 — music, dining, shuffleboard, dancing — but I think we'd all agree that the gigantic iceberg drifting into the waters about 400 miles south of Newfoundland's Grand Banks was probably the most important one, even if most people on board had no idea it was happening.

Similarly, there may be many interesting things going in your job, your family, and your relationships, but if you fail to notice where the giant icebergs (i.e. the Takers in your life) lie, the other stuff becomes kind of academic. Your *Titanic* is going down. All I'm saying is: Look at the big stuff first and the small stuff second.

With that in mind, there are many secondary personality and emotional traits that *affect* the Give/Take scale. But let's focus on what I believe to be the most important of these — the icebergs, so to speak.

I think two influential factors rise above the rest, and I believe these two factors, when looked at along with the Dial, can help us categorize most human beings on the planet. Once categorized, we can then try to figure out whether a person has the potential to change or whether the crocodile is going to remain a crocodile... and we can then plan our own lives accordingly. And by the way, I believe these factors are inborn and not learned.

The Big Two factors are: (1) Energy Level (High/Medium/Low); and (2) Intelligence Level (High/Medium/Low)

I believe that when we weigh these two factors along with a person's position on the Dial, we get a decently accurate picture of that person's basic orientation in life. That's been my experience in the thousands of relationships I've been part of. I think of it as the 3 + 3 + 3 Formula:

- Which of the three types of person is s/he?
- What is his/her basic intelligence level — high, medium, or low?
- What is his/her basic energy level — high, medium, or low?

Energy Level

I believe all human beings operate at a personal energy level that remains more or less constant throughout their lives. Some people have high energy; others have low energy; and still others are in the middle. Though energy level can be influenced by things like diet, exercise, and sleep, I do think most people are high energy, mid energy, or low energy by nature:

High-energy = active; low-energy = passive.

A high-energy person is a doer, an active participant in most situations. The high-energy person wants to be busy and to have an effect on his environment. He wants to be actively playing the game, not warming the bench.

A high-energy person isn't comfortable at rest, but prefers to stay in motion. She wants to get things done. She wants to control outcomes and situations. She has a plan and is working it. She sees life as a creative enterprise, a participatory experience. She wants to leave a footprint behind her.

High-energy people are great to team up with *when* they share your goals. They're the people who help organizations succeed and who change the world through the actions they take. They invent things, start businesses, innovate in the creative arts, and push political change. They are the Type-A personalities.

On the downside, high-energy people can be dangerous when their goals run counter to ours. They don't give up, and if they think we represent an obstacle, they will actively try to remove us. A high-energy enemy is not a good thing to have.

Low-energy people are passive rather than active. They tend to be the passengers rather than the drivers in life. They don't usually take initiative; they will instead allow themselves to be pulled into the plans of high-energy people. They may *join* organizations, but they rarely start them or run them. They tend to play supportive roles that don't require their constant attention and activity.

Low-energy people don't necessarily see it as their sacred duty to go out and change the world every day. They are more prone to accept the cards life deals them. On the other hand, they are less likely to make costly mistakes than high-energy people, because they take fewer risks. They are not necessarily *negative* by nature, but they can be easily defeated by obstacles. Low-energy people tend to procrastinate and wait for others to make key decisions.

When considered along with a person's position on the Dial, energy level makes a huge difference in how that person will manifest Giving or Taking tendencies.

High-Energy Givers:

- Reach out to others they think are in need
- Play active roles in — or initiate — charity efforts
- Participate actively in their loved ones' lives, pushing and pulling to make things better

- Actively seek out problems that need solving

Low-Energy Givers:

- Help when asked, but don't go around offering help
- Write checks to charities, but don't travel to Darfur to lend a hand
- Have a laissez-faire approach to loved ones' lives, but are ready to give time and energy when needed
- Allow others to come up with the solutions, then offer support

High-Energy Takers:

- Scheme and invent new ways to Take from others
- Manipulate systems to wring advantage out of them
- Research existing laws/rules and find creative ways to get around them
- At the extreme end of the Dial, actively rob, murder, rape, and wage wars of conquest

Low-Energy Takers:

- Let others take care of them
- Collect government checks for as long as they can get away with it
- May aid and abet criminals but won't come up with ambitious criminal schemes on their own
- Cheat, lie, and deceive in passive ways

Intelligence Level

While energy level is very important, intelligence is the second main factor that has a strong affect on the nature of one's Giving and Taking.

Nowadays it has become politically incorrect to speak out loud about intelligence. We prefer to pretend that all of us are basically equal in this regard. This is particularly evident in our schools. We have become so concerned with mainstreaming and creating equal opportunity for everyone that we seem to have lost the ability to talk about the 800-pound purple gorilla that's sitting in the middle of the room, playing with a Rubik's Cube: Some people are smart and some people are not. Sorry, but it has to be said.

Bright people are capable of accomplishing much more — in certain areas of life — than people who are not so bright. Intelligence is a very real consideration, and we do ourselves a great disservice as a society by failing to identify it and maximize it in our young people. (We put much more emphasis these days on making sure the not-so-bright get every possible advantage — at school and in the workplace — than we do on challenging and nurturing the best brains among us. The not-surprising result: mediocrity.)

A person's intelligence level goes a long way toward determining the kind of Giving and Taking s/he can and will engage in. Intelligent people are capable of planning and executing much more complex actions than not-so-intelligent people. If we fail to factor in a person's intelligence, we can't get an accurate picture of the potential benefit or danger they represent.

High-Intelligence Givers:

- Come up with innovative ways to benefit society
- Create businesses and works of art that break new ground
- Innovatively improve existing organizations so that Giving is maximized
- Creatively solve social problems

Low-Intelligence Givers:

- May be good at doing "heart" work
- Can be good caregivers and loving, capable parents
- Can be great volunteer workers when given clear objectives
- Can easily be conned by high-intelligence Takers into channeling their good impulses in not-so-great ways

High-Intelligence Takers:

- Can outsmart systems and stay one step ahead of Givers
- Can con and manipulate others very effectively
- Devise complex, clever, and creative schemes

- Can create and lead organized efforts geared toward evil

Low-intelligence Takers:

- Tend to join forces with high-intelligence Takers, playing subordinate roles
- Use physical force and blunt threats to get their way
- Often get caught and end up in jail
- Pack together in groups, as they are typically avoided by others

In a moment, we'll take a look at how some of these combinations of traits come together in distinct types of people. First, though, I'd like to discuss a couple of lesser traits that are worthy of mention in the Give/Take game: lawfulness and introversion/extraversion.

Lawfulness and Introversion

LAWFULNESS

For reasons we won't get into here, some people, on both the Giving side and the Taking side of the Dial, adopt lawfulness (i.e. playing by the established rules) as a constant guide to their behavior, while others do not. Needless to say, this can affect the kinds of Giving and Taking they will engage in.

Lawful does not necessarily equate with good; it simply means a preference for playing within the rules. Some extreme Takers manage to do very nasty, immoral deeds without ever technically breaking the law. A classic example might be a small-town police chief who operates his department like a medieval fiefdom, rewarding those who help him and punishing those who don't. In other cases, lawful Takers simply change the law so as to *make* their actions legal. We've seen many of them who do things like:

- Use state armies to exact their will on others
- Use their government or corporate positions to personally benefit themselves and their friends
- Manufacture shoddy and dangerous (but not illegal) products

- Dupe investors out of money via misleading (but not totally false) claims
- Treat their families with verbal and emotional (but not physical) abuse

Within a marriage, a lawful Taker might avoid having an extramarital affair, *per se*, but might spend endless hours flirting online, looking at porn, and going to strip clubs. Within a business, a lawful Taker might avoid stealing company property outright, but might spend hours of every workweek sleeping in a back office or using his paid work time to write personal emails or to gamble or play games online.

Lawless does not equate with bad, either. Gandhi and Martin Luther King, for example, were willing to step outside the law to accomplish their goals. Some people feel that when the rules get in the way of the greater good, it's justifiable and necessary to step outside of them. Many a great hero has taken this road of action.

INTROVERT VS. EXTRAVERT

Another shaper of Give/Take behavior is a person's degree of outer-directedness versus inner-directedness. Is the person an extravert or an introvert? This factor is *related* to energy level, but it is not exactly the same.

Introverts and extraverts behave in very different ways. An extraverted Taker goes after his quarry directly and openly. An introverted Taker will usually use more passive, indirect, or covert means.

An extraverted extreme Taker might be a conman, a politician, a charismatic organizer, or even an outright mugger or murderer. An introverted extreme Taker might be a computer hacker, an embezzler, a terrorist planner, or a pedophile or other type of "secret" abuser.

On the Giving side, an extraverted extreme Giver might be a religious leader, a government crusader, a public organizer, or a high-profile philanthropist. An introverted extreme Giver might be an anonymous donor, a ghostwriter of inspirational books, a monk, or a tireless legislator who works behind the scenes.

You get the general idea.

Putting It Together

Now let's take a spin around the Dial, using these new factors to get a quick picture of the kinds of "people profiles" we might encounter in life. We'll see what happens when we blend together some of the above traits in random samplings.

Starting at the mild end of the Taking side:

10:00 –12:00 on the Dial (Mild to Moderate Takers)

A Low-Energy, Low-Intelligence Taker at the Mild end of this range might simply be a passive type who needs a lot of direction. As we get closer to the Moderate 10 o'clock mark, though, a low-Energy, low-Intelligence Taker might be someone who acts as if the world owes him a living. He may not be a great contributor at work and may engage in passive behaviors in order to find ways to get the system to Take care of him. Someone in this range might "ride" an injury longer than necessary, in order to collect insurance money, or become a long-term collector of benefits. He may sap family members of resources.

A High-Energy, High-Intelligence Taker in the Moderate range will constantly be looking for competitive advantage. He might start his own business, but will run it without a strong moral framework — always looking to gain the upper hand, without paying much attention to the "collateral damage" he may be doing or the ethical corners he may be cutting. Profit for profit's sake without regard for creating value will be his operating mode. But he won't usually stray into criminality, and he may have a charitable side as well.

8:00 – 10:00 on the Dial (High Takers)

A High-Energy, Low-Intelligence Taker in the High range of the Taking Dial might be someone who actively harms, robs, and bullies other people. He's not much of a planner, but he's got a hateful, disrespectful view of his fellow man and he wants what he wants, when he wants it. Jails are filled with High-Energy, Low-Intelligence Takers. They use angry, blunt force to get what they want.

Flipping it around, a *Low-Energy, High Intelligence Taker,* with introverted tendencies, might be the type to come up with computer scams to rob people or might sell company or government secrets for profit. He'll look for secretive and passive ways to do what a robber would do face-to-face. He could still be a pretty evil person, though.

6:00 – 8:00 on the Dial (Extreme Takers)

As we get closer to 6:00, the Extreme end of the Dial, we find the true psychopaths and sociopaths.

A *High-Energy, Low-Intelligence Taker* in this range is likely to be an outright rapist, child molester, or murderer, Taking what he wants without regard for the rights of his victims.

A *High-Energy, High-Intelligence Taker* at this end of the Dial might be someone who comes up with a clever *plan* to get away with pedophilia on a regular basis. He might be a Hannibal Lecter type, to use a fictional reference, or, if he's Lawful, he might be an Uday Hussein who used government structures to "legally" conduct organized rapes of females within the Iraqi school system. In history, we have many examples of *High-Energy, High-Intelligence Takers* whose Taking took on global proportions — Genghis Khan, Attila the Hun, Alexander the Great, Adolph Hitler. We tend to view these people as Good or Evil depending upon our cultural orientation.

An extreme *Low-Energy, High-Intelligence Taker,* with an introverted leaning, might be someone like a Ted Kaczynski, the famed "Unabomber" who lived alone in a rural shack, covertly using his high intelligence to destroy lives. A Lawful type with the same attributes might concoct malicious computer viruses for his own amusement, without crossing the line to crime or murder.

On the Giving side of the Dial:

12:00 – 2:00 on the Dial (Mild to Moderate Givers)

A *Low-Energy, High-Intelligence Giver* at the Mild to Moderate range of the

Dial would be a positive contributor to a team who might provide good ideas for higher-energy team members to act upon. His contribution will be intellectual rather than action-oriented, his commitment verbal rather than physical. He may be a passive charity donor and might come up with creative ideas for raising money, though he probably won't put those ideas into action.

By contrast, the *High-Energy, Low-Intelligence Giver* will make a great "recruit" to a cause. S/he will man the telephones and go door-to-door, providing the manpower that the above person may not.

2:00 – 4:00 on the Dial (High Givers)

In the High Giving range people adopt causes with strong belief and commitment. A *High-Energy, High-Intelligence Giver* at this Dial setting might start a charity organization or at least agree to chair one. S/he will come up with creative new ideas to generate money for the charity.

A *Low-Energy, Low-Intelligence Giver* at this level might be someone who donates a good amount of money to a cause and prays for its success, but doesn't invest action, thought, and energy. On a creative or business team, this person will be a positive emotional influence and will pitch in when invited to do so, but won't have a lot of ideas or muscle to contribute.

A *High-Energy, Low-Intelligence Giver* at the 3/4 o'clock level, by contrast, will be an aggressively positive person who probably believes strongly in a cause or religion. This person is at risk for being taken advantage of. S/he has a lot of positive energy to contribute but lacks good intellectual discernment about what is a truthful, positive cause and what may not be. S/he can be misled into supporting questionable causes.

4:00 – 6:00 on the Dial (Extreme Givers)

As we approach the 6:00 mark, we find the Extreme Giver, who offers total life commitment to a belief or a cause, often to the detriment of family relationships and personal needs.

A *High-Energy, Low-Intelligence Giver* at this range of the Dial is someone who might be described as fanatical. S/he has a passionate level of commitment and dedication, but lacks an intellectual compass. This is the type of person who can be recruited by a fundamentalist cause and can be talked into putting his own life at risk (usually by someone smarter who's not willing to take that risk himself).

A *Low-Energy, High-Intelligence Introverted Giver* at this end of the Dial might be a highly spiritual person who decides to drop out of society and meditate in a cave for eight years, while a *High-Energy, High-Intelligence Extraverted Giver* in the 5/6 o'clock range will tend to be a person who *leads* a religious, social, or political cause. As I've said before, there are a few individuals at the very high end of this range who are true saints and have transcended the normal range of human needs. But there are others at this end of the Dial who become full-time fighters through self-denial and fanaticism. These people Give up everything in the name of a cause and end up burned out, exhausted, and/or paying some kind of deep personal price for their commitment.

So that's a quick look at how these extra factors combine in a pretty simple way to "un-complicate" people. Of course, in reality, not everyone is at a high or low extreme in terms of energy and intelligence; there is a lot of middle ground as well. I just want to give you a general idea, and it's easier to look at the highs and lows. Think about the people in your own life and use the 3 + 3 + 3 Formula. Try to classify them by energy level, intelligence level, and Giving/Taking "score." See if this helps you gain any insight into how to deal with these people or what to expect from them. (If you'd like to see more examples of well-known Givers and Takers, please see the Appendix at the back of the book.)

Next we're going to look at one more important factor: the emotions.

7

Emotions

It is impossible to understand anything about what makes human beings tick without taking emotions into consideration. Emotions guide both our thinking and our behavior. Worried emotions produce worried thoughts and defensive actions; happy emotions produce happy thoughts and carefree actions. Emotions go a long way toward dictating the quality of life that we experience. If we *feel* happy, then we *are* happy, regardless of how much or how little we may materially possess. If we *feel* scared and envious, then no amount of material possessions will give us a truly wealthy life experience.

In fact, it would not be exaggerating to say that over 90 percent of the value we assign to our lives on a daily basis is a result of the emotions we predominantly experience.

Happy emotions can rocket us up into the Give side of the Dial; fearful, angry emotions can plunge us to the depths of the Taking side.

Emotions are primal energies. They precede thought. Emotions are processed in the so-called "mid-brain," which was developed in human beings long before the neocortex, the processor of abstract thoughts. We make most of our decisions in life based on our emotions, even though we manage to convince ourselves we are making them on the basis of logic, experience, and good advice.

Emotions are the great equalizer. No matter what age, race, religion, gender, or nationality you are, you share the same basic set of emotions with the rest of the human race. Emotions are what bridge the gap between a New York banker, a

Siberian shaman, and an Inuit fisherman. A smile is a smile is a smile, and a snarl is a snarl is a snarl.

Although there are countless theories about emotion and countless lists of so-called "primary" emotions, I believe the core list of human emotions comes down to seven, and we'll see how these relate to the Joe Dial in just a moment.

The Seven Primary Emotions

The seven main human emotions are:

1. Joy
2. Love
3. Sadness
4. Surprise
5. Desire
6. Anger
7. Fear

These emotions have different meanings in different people's minds, so let me tell you quickly what I mean by them.

1. Joy is just a happy, positive, optimistic feeling. It is an experience of rightness, satisfaction, and contentment. It includes spiritual joy and material joy. There can be momentary and superficial joy, like the rapture of eating a delicious meal, or deep, abiding joy, like the peace of mind some prisoners-of-war experience despite their horrifying circumstances. Joy is positive energy.

2. By *Love* I mainly mean the powerful affection and sense of care that a person feels for another living being. It includes the love of parent for child, spouse for spouse, and friend for friend. It doesn't specifically include lust, which is covered under *desire*. Love is positive energy.

3. Sadness refers to a whole range of passive "negative" emotions, such as disappointment, emptiness, hurt, disillusionment, and depression. The sadness range of emotions typically occurs when our expectations are shattered in some way. Sadness is negative energy.

4. *Surprise* means the shock of the unexpected. A surprising *event* can be positive or negative, but in the moment you are experiencing it, surprise is just surprise — a jarring reaction to the unexpected. Surprise can be positive or negative energy.

5. *Desire* means the craving for something we don't currently possess. It can include sexual desire, hunger, thirst, and other physical needs. It can also include the desire for higher-level things, such as job satisfaction or love. At the dark end of the desire spectrum is a range of emotions that includes envy, jealousy, greed, and resentment. Desire can be positive or negative energy.

6. *Anger* is pretty much what it sounds like — a strong "negative" reaction projected outward at another living being. At its extreme end it is rage and violence, at its mild end it is annoyance, irritation. Anger is negative energy.

7. *Fear* is a primal and powerful emotion that stems from the threat of possible loss — loss of life, safety, possessions, love, companionship, security, etc. It includes worry, anxiety, guilt, and dread, as well as repulsion and revulsion. Fear is a tremendous negative motivator. Fear is negative energy.

Emotions have great power to catapult us, at least temporarily, into the more extreme ranges of the Dial, both on the Give and Take side. Positive emotions make us feel a whole lot more Giving, while negative emotions can plunge us deep into Take mode.

But emotions can cause more than just a temporary flip of the needle.

Depending upon our basic orientation to life, emotions tend to feed into a *cycle* that produces more of the same emotion. Certain events in life, for example, can ignite a feeling of fear or suspicion: a pink slip on your desk at work, a letter from the IRS in your mailbox, a lipstick stain on your spouse's shirt. If you are a person who tends to live on the fear side of the fence, the fearful emotion will probably trigger a chain of fearful thoughts, which increases the fearful emotion even more, triggering *more* fearful or suspicious thoughts, and so on. This can then produce aggressive, defensive, or self-destructive behavior.

If you are *not* a basically fearful person, then after you experience the initial burst of fear, it will quickly resolve itself into a more productive emotion such as curiosity or resolve.

The same tends to happen with happier emotions. If you receive a piece of optimistic news *and* you are a basically optimistic person, this news can turn your whole day around and make you see the world in a positive light. This experience tends to feed into your optimistic nature and make you even more likely to be optimistic in the future.

If you are basically pessimistic, the same optimistic news might produce a blip of joy, but this will soon be snuffed out by suspicion, distrust, and the assumption that the good news isn't real or meaningful. This, too, feeds back into your basic personality, strengthening and reinforcing it.

Emotion is both cause and effect.

What does this have to do with the Dial? Well, it turns out that each of us tends to experience a certain habitual range of emotions, depending upon where we "live" on the Dial. Though there are seven Primary Emotions, Givers are weighted heavily toward three or four of these, and Takers are weighted heavily toward three or four very different ones.

Giving, Taking, and the Primary Emotions

On a given day, both Givers and Takers will typically experience only three or four of the Primary Emotions most of the time. They will revert to these favored emotions by habit, while experiencing the others only as rare exceptions. And, again, the basic dispositions of Givers and Takers tend to *produce* these habitual emotions, which then loop back and reinforce the dispositions. In this way, emotions both *flow from* and *help to create* the basic Give or Take personality.

Givers tend to experience *joy* and *love* in abundance. For them, life is basically good, and they maintain a positive outlook. They get joy out of trying to help people and by doing the right thing, and they feel love as a primary motive. Because they have a positive charge to their batteries and a full rather than empty orientation in life, they are not usually *driven* by the *desire* emotions, especially envy and jealousy. Rather, they think in terms of what others might need or desire from *them*. They experience anger only on occasional moments on "special days." This usually occurs as a result of being hurt or "Taken" by someone they trusted.

On the *fear* continuum, Givers do experience worry and anxiety, but it is usually related to concerns about loved ones or about their own ability to help those around them. Their inability to save the world produces much distress. Their predominant negative emotion is sadness, which they experience when they have been hurt by someone they trust or when they think they have fallen short of their goals on a given day. They can easily be disappointed in themselves when they think they have let other people down or have allowed someone to take advantage of them. Guilt — another aspect of fear — flows from this.

Surprise happens when their upbeat expectations are shattered. Surprise tends to lead to sadness in Givers.

Extreme Givers can be so locked into positive emotions like love and joy that they are like live bait to Takers, who prey on their upbeat innocence.

Takers, on the other hand, experience primary emotions in the *desire* and *anger* areas. They come at life from a negative, "Fill me up" orientation, so they are focused on the things they *lack* and, therefore, *desire*. They look at situations from a perspective of "What can I get out of this?" Envy and jealousy are powerful motivating forces. Takers feel a good deal of anger and resentment toward anyone who seems to stand in the way of their getting. They do feel joy when they acquire something they want, but this is usually a temporary high, which quickly ebbs as they move on to the next thing on their get list. Love may be present from time to time (often it's more lust than real love), but it is not a sustaining motivator. Takers can, however, feel a loving or love-like sense of responsibility for their families and can take them under their wing.

Takers don't worry in the same way as Givers. That is, they don't worry about *how* they accomplish their goals. Doing the *right* thing is not their chief concern, only doing the *effective* thing. Troubled conscience does not keep extreme Takers awake at night. They do fear getting caught, however, and they also fear counterattacks from those they've injured or cheated. Surprise can trigger deep fear and defensiveness in Takers.

Extreme Takers often venture into criminal territory. They will cheat, lie, and steal or even rape, kill, and torture to get what they want, with no real regard for their victims. These people feel fear and anger at extreme levels and have little or no experience of true love or joy.

This is the real tragedy of Taking. When people become completely wrapped up in Taking for themselves, they fail to experience the highest-level emotions that human beings can feel. In their zeal to rob from others, they rob even more from themselves.

An important point to realize is that as people get higher up on the Dial, either on the Giving or the Taking side, they create a couple of problems for themselves:

1. They lose the ability to understand those on the opposite side of the Dial. This makes it difficult for Givers to have effective dealings with Takers, and vice versa, in family, social, or business situations. Extreme Givers and Extreme Takers are like members of different species, with little common ground.

2. They become stunted in their emotional growth. Human beings are designed to stretch and grow through experiencing all seven of the Primary Emotions. When some of these emotions are habitually choked off, the person does not mature fully. Practice makes perfect, and when we don't get enough practice in dealing with our emotions, we stunt our growth.

Emotions and the T&G Person

This brings us back to the idea of balance. By striving to develop both our Giving side and our Taking side and to live life in the 10:10 Zone, we can experience a much more rewarding and mature mixture of emotions. And by doing so, we can experience a quality of life that is manageable, balanced, and rewarding. Peace is the ultimate result.

How does a Take-and-Give person experience the Primary Emotions? In a fuller, more even-keeled way than either Givers or Takers. He does feel the love and joy that the Giver feels, but he does *not* have the deep valleys of sadness and disappointment that can torment high-level Givers. He is able to harness the motivating force of desire, as Takers do, but his desire does not morph into lust or obsession because he doesn't feel that he is basically lacking anything in life. He does see enough injustice and deceit in the world to be able to experience anger in healthy doses, but he does not *live* from a place of anger. He does experience surprise, but he is not thrown for a loop by it. That's because he knows what to expect better than extreme Givers and Takers do.

In other words, he is able to experience a wide range of emotions, but he is not stuck in the extremes of any single emotion. His experience of fear, for example, is less extreme than that of Givers or Takers. He does not have the worry of failure that can dominate the minds of many dedicated Givers, nor does he stay awake fretting about getting caught or about who might be trying to screw him, as Takers do.

As a result, the Take-and-Give person is seasoned and matured by a wide range of emotions, without being dominated by any one in particular. This allows him to develop into a wise, well-rounded, balanced person, unlikely to be undone by his emotions as both Givers and Takers so often are. As I was writing this section, a news story came to mind as an example. You may recall the famous murder case in which a doctor was tortured and beaten nearly to death, then condemned to listen as his wife and daughter were raped, murdered, and burned in another part of his house. Somehow this remarkable man managed to refrain from taking revenge and, when his court date came around, he was even able to calmly and clearly testify against the men who destroyed his family. Amazingly, this man was able to stay in the 10:10 Zone and do what needed to be done in order to ensure that these extreme Takers got the consequences they had earned. He took an evolutionary stance instead of plunging into the Hurt Zone.

How do we learn to avoid the devastating extremes of emotion and live in the Peace Place instead? It's a tremendous challenge, yes, but it all starts with a clear understanding of the powerful forces we're up against. We have to know what *makes us* Takers and Givers in the first place.

So let's step back for a minute and explore that subject a bit…

8

The Role of "Nature"

What is it that makes us the way we are? How does one person become a high-energy Taker and the next person a low-energy Giver? In my opinion, our Taking and Giving nature is a function of both nature and nurture. That is, some of it is in the genes, and some of it is a result of our very human upbringing. It's truly a mixture of both, and we have to understand the great power of *both* of these influences in order to have a decent shot at changing.

The nature part is what's given to us at birth; it can't be controlled or chosen. Our particular sperm and egg shake hands at the instant of conception and exchange their chromosomes. The genetic dice are rolled, and we are born with a certain predisposition. There's nothing we can do about it.

It's not that we're *determined*, but we do have a strong set of *tendencies* built in. As we get older, we ideally learn to work with our tendencies and become better at *managing* the basic personality we were given, but we can't usually flip from croc to rabbit.

To understand the nature side of the equation, we really have to look at the whole history of humankind, going back to prehistoric times. Many elegant theories about evolution and personality have been proposed by people with impressively long strings of letters after their names, but most of these theories are pretty abstract and hard to grasp, at least for me. They don't pass the gut test. My own version, which might not impress an Oxford anthropology professor, is a lot simpler and easier to understand.

Genes and Food

Our basic nature, I believe, stems from diet — not the diet *we* eat, but the diet our ancestors ate, which is passed down to us in our genes.

We all know that genes play a huge role in controlling the kind of person we become. Genes are passed on from parents to offspring through our chromosomes. Not only do genes control the obvious stuff like height, hair color, and eye color, but they also control some of the subtle inner stuff, like how we behave and what we're good at. In one famous study, for example, musical talent was traced throughout many generations of the Bach family.

Genes also control blood type. There are four basic types of blood: A, B, O, and AB. In Japan, it has long been believed that blood type has a strong influence on personality. It is even reported that Japanese companies use blood type as an important factor in making hiring decisions. In the West, this belief has not had as strong a tradition, but I think the blood-type theory has a lot of merit, whether you believe it literally or just see it as a metaphor for talking about genes.

It all comes down to food.

Food? Yes. Over the ages, the pursuit of food has played a huge role in the development of personality and blood type in humans. It is hard to overstate the importance of this. In my opinion, any theory of personality that does not emphasize the role of food and survival probably doesn't have a lot of merit.

Just hear me out.

When we look at the history of man, all the way back to when *homo* first walked *erectus* (no groans, please), there have been times and places when we relied more on eating meat than eating plants. There have also been times when we relied more on eating plants. Finally, there have been times — as in today's "civilized" world — when we have lived as fairly balanced omnivores. In the world according to Joe, these three food preferences (carnivore, herbivore, and omnivore) correspond *in a very general way* to our three basic personality types of Taker, Giver, and T&Ger.

Let's see how that works.

In those times and places when we ate mostly meat, human beings were forced to survive as predators. Our very facial structure — two eyes on the front of the face, rather than on the sides of the head — identifies us as an essential predator. That's why most animals still run like hell when they see us (smart creatures). When we lived as predators, we had to hunt daily for food. We didn't have fridges, which meant the meat didn't keep for long, so we had to hunt more or less constantly.

Hunting was a very stressful lifestyle. It required being on the go, moving quickly and stealthily, and basically managing life through an anger temperament. Anger had a strong survival value. After all, it's hard to kill a rampaging saber-toothed tiger in a cool, relaxed mood. Surprise was also a common emotion, because attacks and counterattacks often came out of nowhere — like a mother grizzly bear taking exception to our dining on her cubs.

Fear caused adrenalin to course through the body on a daily basis. Not only did hunters have to cope with the stress of finding, tracking, chasing down, and killing food, but they also had to cope with the stress of potentially getting eaten by something with four-inch teeth. The so-called fight-or-flight response developed during our hunting days. The emotion of envy also arose; if we had a bad hunt, we would naturally start eyeing the prey that another hunting party had bagged, just as they would eye ours if the situation was reversed.

As meat-eaters, we were fundamentally Takers. We went after what we wanted, and we took it. And we were always on guard, ready to attack or to turn tail and run. Fear. Anger. Surprise.

In contrast, there have been times and places when we've been able to rely chiefly on plants for our staple diet. Sometimes this was accomplished through gathering and sometimes through agriculture. One striking difference between plant-eating and meat-eating is that a blueberry bush doesn't usually rip your face off when you pick its fruit. Also, grains and other plant-derived foods can be stored much longer than meat. Surpluses could be developed, which carried us over those times when the gathering and harvesting were a little lean. This enabled us to work hard for a period of time, then take it easy for a while and play the lute. Sharing became natural.

All of this added up to a lifestyle that was a good deal less stressful than hunting.

As a general rule, plant-eaters had more of the Giver personality. They were more peaceful, relaxed, and content than hunters. They had bounty to share, and though they did have to watch out for *being* hunted, they didn't put themselves in harm's way every day. Anger didn't have much survival value to them. Rather, a cool, rational, planning approach worked better. They developed a blood type that gave rise to the Givers of today.

Modern Personalities

Over the generations, the mental/emotional states of hunters and plant-eaters have been largely responsible for developing the main personalities of every individual alive today. Some people have a lot of energy and anxiety, while others move very slowly and deliberately. Some take action, while others procrastinate. In my opinion, the carnivorous disposition led to the development of what we call the Type-A personality. This is the sort of person who can't stay still and always needs to be accomplishing something. S/he needs to be "on the go," ready to pounce on any opportunity that arises.

As infants, Type-A's — those who carry more of the carnivore lineage — often require a lot of attention from parents. They have many needs and are not shy about making them known. As adults, they are insecure and nervous, always looking over their shoulders for enemies who want to Take their "meat." They are always searching for "prey," whether that be wealth, mating partners, or political advantage over others.

Conversely, the vegetarian disposition led to today's Type-B personality. These individuals are less prone to worry, more at peace, and more laid-back. They have not inherited stress as a main ingredient in their bloodline. Thus, they tend to be more comfortable in life. They are not immediately suspicious of everyone they meet. They feel connected to others in a positive way, not viewing others as competitors but as cooperators. They inherently recognize the contribution that all people make to "the tribe" (for it was in agricultural societies that true specialization within the workforce arose). Herbivore people are often churchgoers, good neighbors, and active community members. Their chief emotions are joy, love, and sadness.

And then, of course, there are the omnivores. They share some of the traits of both groups. In a world of meat-eaters (Takers) and plant-eaters (Givers), the omnivore is perhaps the best adapted, because he can walk the line between the two groups. Possessing enough of the carnivore to keep himself sharp and well defended, he also has enough of the plant-eater in him to be able trust his fellow man, share his bounty, and relax when the workday is over. He is not as likely to hurt or *be* hurt as pure Takers or pure Givers. The omnivore (T&G person) experiences the full range of human emotions more consistently than does either of the more extreme groups. This allows the T&Ger to mature emotionally at a faster rate and to relate comfortably to both of the other groups.

You might think that by this point in our history, we would *all* have evolved into omnivore personalities, but that's not how genetics works. We'll come back to that in a minute.

But first...

How the Blood Types Mixed

How did plant-eater blood get mixed up with meat-eater blood in the first place? Not by mutual agreement, let's just say.

As meat-eaters packed together to cooperate in hunts (bringing down a mastodon was not a solo effort), they formed small tribes, then larger tribes, and eventually societies and nations. Meat-eaters naturally formed *aggressive* groups, no matter what size those groups were. With all that testosterone and adrenalin boiling in their blood, their basic orientation was one of Taking. Their habit was to conquer and to possess what belonged to other groups. These other groups could be meat-eaters or plant-eaters. Plant-eaters were especially appealing victims, though, because they were easy to conquer and also had great stores of really cool stuff — not to mention the women.

One of the most repellent qualities of the meat-eating conqueror-type has been the practice of rape. Sorry, but it can't be ignored. From the days of the earliest warring tribes to today's warring nations, it has been a custom for men in conqueror groups to rape the women within conquered groups. Greek, Persian, and Roman armies were known to commit such acts, but it was no different in Vietnam or Nazi Germany, nor has it changed in modern-day Sudan. Conquerors routinely kill the men, steal the assets, and rape the women. Though forbidden by international agreements, the practice of wartime rape has continued since the first meat-eating tribe committed its first conquest.

Conquest-rape quite literally mixes the blood of the conqueror with that of the conquered, the aggressive carnivore with the peaceful herbivore. As a result, millions of women throughout history have given birth to offspring of their most feared and hated enemies. Sad as it is, probably every human being alive on Earth has rape in his or her DNA.

Today, of course, mixing of blood happens more often through peaceful means, but the *contrast* between Taker blood and Giver blood still plays out in the daily drama of dancing chromosomes and jousting blood types.

Giver and Taker types are preserved through genetics.

How the Blood Types Are Preserved

Genetics plays an intriguing numbers game that keeps distinct traits alive in the bloodline, while also allowing for some mixing of traits (hybridization) to occur. Maybe you remember ol' Gregor Mendel, the famous monk who experimented with pea plants. You probably learned about him in high school biology; he is considered the father of modern genetics. Basically, he realized that dominant traits and recessive traits of plants and animals combine in a fascinating way that preserves pure traits for future generations while also allowing mixed traits to develop. Put a black cat and a white cat together, and you might expect to get all gray kittens or all black-and-white-spotted kittens, but that's not what happens. In reality, you might get three black-and-white kittens, one pure black kitten, and one pure white kitten. The same thing goes for human traits such as eye color, hair color, size, genetic diseases, and a thousand other factors.

It's complicated, and beyond the scope of this book, but basically nature has devised a mathematical system that keeps pure traits, such as blood type, preserved down through the ages in an unpredictable and seemingly random way. This system ensures that two parents won't have four kids that are all the same. They might, for example, have two kids that are Take-and-Givers, one kid that's a Taker, and one kid that's a Giver.

Genetics preserves the Taker and Giver lines within our DNA, ensuring that these types will continue to keep appearing, both as pure strains and mixed strains. But what does that mean on a practical basis? It means we all must accept the fact that, to a fair extent, crocodiles are still crocodiles and rabbits are still rabbits, and we must learn to deal with both types.

But genetics is not the whole story; that's only the nature side of the equation. There's also the very important nurture side. Parents and society have a huge effect on the Taking and Giving aspects of our children…

9

The Role of "Nurture"

When it comes to raising Givers and Takers, there's no nature *versus* nurture debate. It's a clear case of nature AND nurture. Both are important. One picks up where the other leaves off.

Yes, each of us is born with a powerful charge in our blood as a result of our carnivore/herbivore lineage, but parents, teachers, and society also play a huge role in determining whether we become Takers, Givers, or T&Gers as adults. How *much* influence does nature have versus nurture? There's no set formula; a lot of it depends on how strong the variables are on either side. Someone born with an extreme Taking predisposition is bound to become an adult with at least *some* Taking qualities, regardless of how he is raised. We all know of examples of criminal Takers who come from Giving, responsible families. These so-called black sheep may be raised perfectly well, but they just don't turn out as society would hope. Similarly, history is full of stories of saint-like individuals who emerge from the darkest of upbringings.

On the other hand, environment does have an enormous influence, and it works according to a very simple formula. That is, if you Give a child more than is healthy to Give, you put him/her in a position of Taking most of the time. Thus, you give the child more practice at Taking than Giving and train the child to be a Taker. We see this in the case of both spoiled rich kids and public assistance-addicted, low-income kids (though income itself has nothing to do with it). It is a simple case of too much receiving and not enough Giving back.

It works the other way, too. When parents Take too much from a child, as in the case of undependable, alcoholic, immature, or drug-addicted parents who rely on their kids to handle the adult responsibilities of the household, they raise kids who know how to take care of everyone but themselves. They can Give, but they can't Take.

So, again, it's a question of degree. If a child is raised in an extreme Taking-centric environment, s/he is likely to lean toward being a Taker, regardless of his/her genetic leanings, and vice versa.

Creating Balance and Imbalance

It is our responsibility — not only as parents, but as a society — to create the right balance of Taking and Giving for our young people, so that they can mature into adults with a healthy mix of Take and Give in their personalities. This healthy mix of T&G equips children with the emotional and mental structure required to be good and moral citizens. Children trained to be extreme Takers or extreme Givers, on the other hand, are unlikely to mature into balanced T&Gers. It's really that simple.

Throughout our lives, especially as children, we need to receive the right set of expectations and instructions from our society in order to develop a good balance of Give and Take in our lives. Our parents are the main parties responsible for providing this, but extended families, neighbors, schools, and government systems must do their part as well. If we want to raise citizens who live in the 10:10 Zone, we must create families *and* social/government structures that encourage healthy development.

I believe there is a ladder of developmental needs that must be met in order to produce a healthy individual with a good mix of Give and Take. When these needs are met in a balanced fashion, the ladder stands straight and tall, and the individual grows up in the 10:10 Zone. When the needs are not met in a balanced fashion, the Ladder of Life leans (or maybe even topples) to one side or the other, Give or Take. Most often, this unsteadiness throws us into the negative side of the Dial.

The ladder extends throughout our lives, from birth to death. Of course, the most critical needs occur when we are young, but it does not stop there. We continue to be influenced toward Taking or Giving our entire lives. Society plays a strong role in this.

The "Ladder of Life"

The Ladder of Life looks something like this:

NEGATIVELY CHARGED		POSITIVELY CHARGED
	Death	
Selfish Concerns		Selfless Service
No Contribution		Contribution Expected
No Respect	Senior Years	Respect
"Where's Mine?"		"How Can I Serve?"
Entitlement		Self-Determination
Following		Leadership
Imitation	Middle Age	Creativity / Originality
Taking Relationships		Giving Relationships
Unfair Rewards		Fair Rewards
Dependency	Adulthood	Self-sufficiency
Materialism		Higher Values
Bad Cultural Influences		Good Cultural Influences
Coddling	Adolescence	Risk
Privileges Given		Privileges Earned
No Moral Education		Moral Education
Poor Modeling	Childhood	Good Modeling
Neglect		Caring
Chaos	Infancy	Safety & Predictability
	Birth	

This is not a precise or complete psychological model by any means, but it gives us a general idea to work from. It shows some of the basic needs that *family and society* must fulfill, as well as some of the expectations that must be required *of individuals* in order for individuals to grow into balanced adults with a healthy leaning toward the Giving side. To the extent that the needs and expectations are fulfilled more on right side of the ladder, we raise balanced individuals with a healthy Giving nature. To the extent that the ladder tips more to the left side, we tend to raise Takers.

The way of the world right now, unfortunately, is that we are leaning more toward creating Takers, from birth to death.

Let's look at how it is *supposed* to work, though, using the Ladder of Life as our reference.

Infancy and Childhood

Raising kids is the toughest job on Earth, and no one gets it 100 percent right. The challenge is to raise our children with kindness and compassion, mixed with a healthy dose of expectations and demands. The problem is that kids' needs change as they age, and we, as parents, must accordingly and dynamically change along with them. This is where a lot of us screw up. Childhood begins with a need for the parents to provide total safety and comfort (pure Taking on the part of the child); it ends with a need for parents to take the safety net *away* and allow the child to experience risk and responsibility (increased Giving on the part of the child).

Let's start at the bottom of the Ladder.

At the start of life, babies have a powerful need for *Safety and Predictability*. They need to know that their environment will be comfortable, nurturing, and lacking in unpleasant surprises. They need to be able to count on Mom to respond to their signals of need — to feed them, change their diapers, keep them warm, love them, comfort them, and put them to sleep when they're tired. *Caring* goes hand in hand with this. Infancy is a period of pure Take on the infant's part and pure Give on the part of the parents. If the parents are needy themselves and stuck in Taking mode, as teenaged parents or emotionally immature parents often are, they will not be able to provide constant Caring and Safety to their child.

If the child does not receive predictable Safety and Caring and is exposed to *Neglect* and *Chaos* instead, she will become stuck in Need and will always be a Taker. Why? Because she will not trust the world around her to provide for her. Fear of deprivation will become a dominant emotion. She'll always be nervous about not having enough.

As the child grows, there is an increased need for *Good Modeling* on the part of the parents. The parents must not only care for the *child*, but also demonstrate care and respect for one another, for the child's siblings, and for the world at large. They must also model fairness, ethics, morality, and a good balance of Give and Take. If the parents *tell* the child one thing but model something else (i.e. "Do as I say, not as I do"), the child will quickly learn that how the parents *act* is more important than what they say. Parents who are Takers in life can't help but model Taking, and children learn what is modeled more than what is taught.

Still, teaching is important too. Children need a *Moral Education*, a solid grounding in what is right and wrong and why. Parents must be willing to serve as living examples to their kids *and* to explain to their kids why they make the choices they do — a demanding job if ever there was one. If parents are Takers themselves, they will be too lazy to undertake such a daunting challenge, and the kids will learn Taking only.

As kids continue to age, parents, teachers and society must shift away from total Caring to an expectation that the child will Give something in return — effort, work, personal responsibility. *Privileges Earned* become more important than privileges Given. Once the child is past the age of reason, parents must expect regular contributions from him. If an older child continues to be Given everything, without having to Give anything in return, he learns only Taking mode.

Finally, as kids approach and enter the teen years, the parents must begin to allow them to take some *Risk*. Children need to experience mild levels of "danger" in order to mature into adults. Of course, we don't want to put our kids into stupidly dangerous situations, but we do want to let them test their independence and go without the parental safety net from time to time. Only a child who trusts himself can become a Giver, and self-trust is learned through *our* trust. When we allow our child to take a risk, we are saying, "I trust you to overcome this obstacle and to do the right thing."

Childhood begins with total safety and ends with much of that safety being removed.

Adolescence

When adolescence kicks in, children begin to seriously experiment with becoming adults. It is important, at this stage, that they be steered toward forming good life values. Here is where many young people go astray because they follow shallow, negative role models. We need to offer our kids *Good Cultural Influences.* Violent rap music and realistic videogames that simulate murder and destruction, for instance, can be highly detrimental to an adult-in-training. A little of this won't destroy a kid, but a lot will. *Bad Cultural Influences* need to be heavily counterbalanced by good ones. Similarly, a little *Materialism* is fine and natural (every young person loves cool stuff), but pop culture's emphasis on collecting "bling," cars, "b*tches," and power is horribly misguided. Adolescence is a critical time for adopting *Higher Values* such as compassion, personal responsibility, and a desire to make the world a better place.

Adulthood and Middle Age

As we climb the Ladder of Life into adulthood, *Self-Sufficiency* needs to be rewarded, both by our parents and by society at large. To the extent that we reward *Dependence* by Giving people things they do not earn, we keep them locked in the

Taking modes of childhood and adolescence. The more we Give and the less we require of young adults, the more we create extended adolescence and groom our young adults to be Takers.

As adults enter the work force, *Fair Rewards* are important. The young person must feel amply and fairly compensated for his work and must also know that the financial reward is tied to his level of productivity. He must be paid well enough to take pride in his work and to feel motivated to work hard. On the other hand, he shouldn't ever be paid at a higher level than his contribution merits. In Socialist Russia, for example, there was no clear connection between contribution and reward. Basic laws of nature were disregarded. Thus, there was little motivation to be productive on the job and instead, a Taking motivation dominated the work force. To the extent that we in the U.S. bend over backwards to ensure equality of pay without regard for excellence of results, we do the same thing to our work force.

As adults age, we should expect them to shift more and more toward a *Giving* orientation in all of their relationships: work, family, and community. This is the message we should send to all adults in society. If we have trained our young adults to be chiefly Takers, though, they will have a hard time making the transition to being good parents, business owners, managers, and public servants, for these are roles in which a Giving, adult attitude is crucial.

Middle age is the period in which most adults normally peak in terms of their Giving. This is a time to assert one's *Creativity/Originality* and contribute one's unique talents, as opposed to only *Imitating* others. Similarly, it is a time to show *Leadership* in at least some areas of life, instead of only *Following*. In middle age, the Giving-oriented adult will experience a sense of *Self-Determination* and control over his/her destiny, while the Taking adult will have a feeling of *Entitlement* and will complain of feeling cheated or "screwed" by life. The dominant question in the Middle Age of a Giving-oriented adult should be, *"How Can I Serve?"* rather than *"Where's Mine?"*

Senior Years

We continue to train adults to be Takers or Givers well into the Senior Years. The last decades of life can be an enormously important Giving period... or not. It depends on what we expect and demand.

It all starts with *Respect*. In some families and societies, elderly people are greatly respected. This respect is reflected in the fact that elders are expected to continue *Contributing* to society at a high level. Their wisdom and guidance is eagerly sought in family and business decisions. In other societies (such as our own, sadly), elders are put out to pasture and no longer expected or encouraged to contribute. Thus, they are turned into low-level Takers, concerned mainly with protecting their benefits and their fixed incomes. Why? Because we have deprived them of their Giving position.

Ideally, a senior citizen would devote at least some of her life to *Selfless Service*. Since most elders no longer need to earn as much as they did during their peak productive years, they can become ideal contributors to organizations that need management and manpower but are low on funds. Seniors can be great consultants, teachers, coaches, and mentors, drawing from their vast experience and knowledge to help others succeed. *Or* they can become cantankerous, self-centered care recipients focused only on Earth-shattering issues like whether today's dessert is going to be the lime or the raspberry Jell-o. It all depends on what we, as a society, expect, encourage, and allow.

By offering a healthy set of instructions and expectations—the Ladder of Life—from birth to death, we can nurture balanced Giving in mankind. We can't compensate for every Taking trait that Nature builds in, but we can shift the trajectory of evolution in a positive and productive direction.

Over-Nurturing and Under-Nurturing

It's my belief that we are currently moving in the wrong direction as a society. We seem to be doing a masterful job of both under- and over-nurturing our kids and our citizens, and in so doing, we are creating a present and future generation of Takers.

We create an *under*-nurturing scenario when we enable young people who have not grown out of the Taking stage themselves to have children. These young parents have often been raised to be Takers and have not yet matured into the Giving phase of adulthood. As a result, they are unable to really nurture *their* infants and young children, thus setting them off on the wrong foot for life.

We're *over*-nurturing by providing too much stuff and too many privileges to people who haven't earned them. This includes our kids and, in many cases, our adult citizens. When we over-nurture people, we do them a grave disservice. We tell them their Giving is not required and that they are entitled to everything they need without earning it or even asking for it.

When people no longer have to ask for help and feel they can simply fill out an anonymous Entitlement Form simply because they exist, a monkey wrench is thrown into the natural laws of Giving and Taking — something we'll discuss in the next chapter.

10

Striking the Right Balance

So here's the dilemma:

We want to create families, workplaces, and social institutions that are more oriented toward Giving than Taking, right? But the challenge is: How do we do this without causing collateral damage and creating more Takers? After all, if we become more Giving as parents, teachers, and governments, won't we groom the recipients of our Giving to become Takers? Yes and no. It's a tricky question and the subject of this chapter and the next.

First, let's look at the ideal Giving state we all want to strive for.

How to Live in the Peace Place: The 60/40 Rule

We don't want to live in a society of Takers. Rather, we want to live in a Giving-oriented culture. We want the majority of our citizens to be focused on what they're contributing to, rather than extracting from, their families, their jobs, and the system.

I talked in an earlier chapter about living in the Peace Place of the 10:10 Zone. People who live in the Peace Place have their Dial needles hovering at around two o'clock on the Dial. They are adept at both Giving and Taking but spend most of their time on the Giving side of the Dial.

The Peace Place is the ideal range to live in, both personally and as members of society. When we are in the Peace Place, we *lean* toward Giving without being compulsive about it. Our general orientation is always positive rather than negative. We are always thinking more about what we *bring* to the table of life rather than what we Take away in our doggie bag, although we are also wise enough and balanced enough to Take when the time is right.

That's the way we *want* to be. But how do we get there?

The main way is to practice the 60/40 Rule, which I hinted at earlier. That is, keep about 60 to 70 percent of your focus, day in and day out, on what you are Giving, contributing, and bringing to the table. Keep only 30 to 40 percent of it, at most, on what you are receiving. If you make a habit of using this one simple "master formula," I guarantee you will transform all of your life relationships into positive ones.

When *all* parties in a relationship use the 60/40 Rule, that's when real magic happens.

- When both a husband and a wife spend 60 percent of their time and attention on helping, supporting, and caring for the other, a great marriage is born.
- When two friends each strive to do 60 percent of the listening, 60 percent of the supporting, 60 percent of the activity-planning, and 60 percent of the beer-buying, great lifetime friendships are launched.
- When every employee of a company focuses at least 60 percent of their energy on what they're contributing rather than what they're getting back, great business successes come about.
- When most of the citizens of a country take to heart John F. Kennedy's advice to "Think not what your country can do for you, but what you can do for your country," a truly great nation is born.

Unfortunately, that's not the nation or the world we live in right now. We live in a Taking-heavy world in which:

- Many parents have children primarily to fulfill *themselves* or to collect more government benefits. Sad but true.

- Citizens look to the government as a *provider of resources*.
- People get married in order to have their own emotional needs met and then bail out as soon as any sacrificing effort is required.
- Young adults enter the workplace with a "Pay me" attitude rather than humility, dedication, and an eagerness to learn.
- Employers treat employees like expendable resources, wringing all the work and creativity out of them, then downsizing in order to make a quarterly profit.
- Neighbors act like feuding warlords rather than cooperative friends.
- Sports heroes refuse to play to their full potential whenever there's a minor issue with their multi-zillion-dollar contracts.
- Spoiled, superficial Takers are celebrated and emulated on reality TV shows and in the print media.
- Politicians have become ego-accelerated Takers who view public office as a lucrative career move rather than a period of selfless public service.
- Many of the wealthiest citizens no longer make their money by *creating* value, but by *Taking* value — through buying other companies, breaking them up, and selling them off, or through "shorting" stock or otherwise using their energy to Take companies down rather than build them up.

We need to return to a Giving-heavy mindset in every aspect of our lives. It's the only approach that makes sense. Right now, as I look around, I see the reverse. I see the *40/60* Rule instead — everyone seems to be a little (or a lot) more concerned about what they're getting than what they're Giving, producing, contributing, or sharing. The energy meter of the population is pulling toward the negative zone, big time.

The result? An economy in recession. Less wealth to go around for everyone. An atmosphere of fear, distrust, and "I, me, mine." An obsession with getting our personal piece of the pie.

But when we flip the formula around to 60/40 on the Give side, the pie itself gets bigger! There's more for all of us! We all benefit! Not only do we get to sleep at night feeling the peace of being contributors, Givers, and producers, but more *material* wealth comes our way, too. What goes around truly does come around, and as ye Give, truly do ye receive. In fact, the surest way to receive *is* to Give. Think about it. Would *you* rather Give to a Giver or a Taker?

That's what's funny about selfishness: It doesn't even work from a *selfish* perspective! When we're focused mainly on what we're getting, we're reluctant to be fully productive. Wary of being shortchanged, we refuse to throw ourselves 100 percent into our companies, our teams, our relationships. Fearful of being asked to Give more than our fair share, we hold back and contribute only grudgingly, waiting for the next opportunity to Take. The result is a net loss for all of us — *especially* ourselves, for we rob ourselves of the ultimate reward of Giving fully of who we are. Working from a negative, "Give me" orientation, we don't even reach our full *individual* potential.

On the other hand, when we work together from a positive orientation (i.e. everyone using the 60/40 Rule), we create vastly more opportunity, wealth, and value for all of us, collectively and individually.

A 60/40 society would represent an enormous evolutionary leap over what we currently have. If you remember nothing else from this book, I would encourage you to practice the 60/40 Rule in all areas of your life.

But now here comes the tricky part. What does the 60/40 Rule mean in *practical* terms? Does it mean we just open our pockets and share our wealth? Won't that create more Takers? Do we write a blank check to every person or cause we see as needy?

No! Not at all. Having a Giving *mindset* is not the same thing as throwing fifties around like confetti or hosting an open bar every night of the week. This is where a lot of confusion creeps in, where a lot of generous-minded people are steered astray. They confuse Giving with open-ended *lavishing*. *True* Giving is not about indiscriminately opening our wallets, literally or figuratively.

Perhaps this little anecdote will help illustrate the point...

The Garden

A guy decides to plant a garden in his back yard. He wants to do it right, so reads up on garden design and builds all these cute little terraces and flowerbeds. He researches flower varieties and plants a nice mix of annuals and perennials. He adds some flowering bushes and ornamental trees. Soon, his garden starts to grow and, sure enough, it's a thing of beauty. A little piece of paradise. A perfect place to enjoy a cup of tea at the end of a long day. The birds and the bees seem to appreciate it, too. Songbirds drop by to serenade the gardener and sing their thank-yous.

The guy decides he wants to attract *even more* birds, so he puts up a dozen bird feeders throughout the garden, which he stocks with sunflower seeds and other birdie treats. The feeders do the trick. More birds *do* start coming, only now it's not just the occasional songbird, but jays and crows and sparrows too. They start fighting and screeching all around the feeders.

Pretty soon, cracked birdseed is being spread all over the place, making a mess on the ground and causing a bunch of unwanted weeds and plants to grow. The squirrels start showing up, drawn by the lure of easy fodder. The chipmunks move in, too, and start burrowing under the garden to build their new homes near the food supply.

Before long, the hawks and foxes catch on to the fact that there's a steady supply of fresh chipmunk steak on hand, and they start showing up, too, along with raccoons, mice, and rats. These creatures bring ticks and fleas and parasites that destroy some of the flowers.

As you've probably guessed, before long, the guy's garden has turned into a chaotic, smelly, noisy mess. There are bird droppings everywhere, and the perfect balance has been destroyed.

So what happened to our would-be gardener's plans of paradise?

Well, what happened was the guy interfered with the natural order of things. By Giving birdseed away too freely, he interrupted the law of cause and effect. You see, birds are supposed to *work* to get their food, and predators are supposed to *work* to track their prey according to the ancient laws of the forest. But by providing an endless supply of clean, prepared, freely available birdseed, he changed the rules of the game. No longer did seed need to be *earned* by tracking it down and carefully extracting it from plants, and no longer did it need to be eaten conservatively or appreciatively — there was a virtually endless supply. No longer did the hawks and the foxes need to *hunt* for their prey; they could now just sit and *wait* for it. The birds even forgot to migrate for the winter. The delicate balance of nature was tipped on its side.

By following the noble instinct to Give, the misguided garden-builder created a Taker's paradise, which soon turned into Hell for all concerned.

Sound familiar?

Interrupting *Human* Nature

This is exactly what we do when we Give indiscriminately to our fellow man. We interrupt the basic laws of nature. In the natural order of things, people are supposed to *earn* their basic requirements of life: food, shelter, clothing, and energy. Earning means working to produce something of value. Producing is a valuable human accomplishment in and of itself, but the *need* to produce in order to survive also provides the *motivation* for us to learn a wide range of important things, such as:

- Trades and job skills
- Personal responsibility
- Interpersonal skills
- Communication skills
- Financial planning
- Character
- Budgeting
- Negotiating skills
- Grooming skills

- Ethics and etiquette
- Energy management
- How to honor commitments
- How to set optimistic but realistic goals
- How to set and attain high standards
- How to work hard and accomplish things

...just to name a few. The motive to earn and produce lies at the base of an enormous *flowchart* of important skills and life lessons. These are the very skills that shape us into solid citizens and valued family members. Without these skills, we remain nonproductive, dependent children, with nothing to offer. Take away the motive to *earn*, and you take away a huge percentage of what is valuable in human life.

When we freely Give to our children and our citizens without granting them the opportunity — and it *is* an opportunity, not a burden — to earn it for themselves, we rob them of the ability to grow and mature into citizens of value. We rob their lives of balance, just as the gardener robbed his garden of balance. We rob them of self-esteem, fulfillment, pride of accomplishment, and a sense of purpose in life.

Freebies teach nothing, for they don't *require* anything of the recipient. A reward is only perceived as a reward if one has to work, struggle, and/or grow to achieve it. The recipient does not value a reward received simply on the basis of need, with no price paid for it.

What Is Free Is Not Appreciated

Here's an inarguable fact about human beings:

Anything that is freely and easily available to us is not appreciated or even acknowledged. That's just the way our brains are constructed. We take for granted whatever we don't have to work for. Think about water, for example.

We need water to live. Water is vitally important to us. Water, in a very real sense, is life itself. It is the most precious commodity on Earth. But water is also freely available everywhere, in virtually every home and workplace. A drink of water costs nothing or next to nothing (unless you buy it in designer bottles).

So when was the last time you felt deeply appreciative of water? When was the last time you gave water a second thought?

And yet, what if you were lost in the desert and had no water? What would your attitude be then? What if you heard about an oasis thirty miles away and decided to make your way there on foot, in the blazing heat? What if you arrived there, barely alive, nursing a snakebite and a broken ankle, and discovered a spring of fresh, cool water? How do you think you would feel about water then? I suspect you might appreciate it quite a bit.

I'm not saying everything in life needs to be so hard won, but I am pointing to the obvious fact that whenever something is placed under our noses, without any effort required, it is taken for granted. It is no longer even *noticed.* That's just our nature as human beings. Our brains are wired to ignore the "givens." We only pay attention to that which requires *effort* to possess.

So when I talk about Giving, I hope you can see that I do not mean handing someone something for nothing, especially not doing so as a thoughtless habit or routine. For when we do that, we *institutionalize* Giving — like our friend with the garden did — and we mess up not only the lives of the recipients themselves, but of all of the residents of "the garden."

True Giving must meet higher standards…

11

Guidelines for True Giving

Giving, then, is about more than just opening our wallets in a knee-jerk fashion. Sure, *sometimes* that's the right thing to do. If you meet someone who is truly cold, hungry, or in need of roadside assistance, you should certainly Give that person whatever they need to relieve their immediate problem, no strings attached. Offering gifts freely and spontaneously to our children, loved ones, and perfect strangers is an important part of life. Helping out when misfortune strikes is a crucial aspect of being human. I certainly don't mean to discourage Giving out of honest generosity or in response to real need, but we do need to be careful.

Free-form Giving can easily devolve into the kind of mistake our gardening friend made. By Giving indiscriminately, he threw a monkey wrench into the laws of nature. We can easily ruin our garden as he did.

Fortunately, there are some Guidelines we can follow to keep us on track. When we observe these Guidelines, we are able to freely practice the 60/40 rule without contradiction and without worrying that we are creating more Takers. In fact, when we follow these Guidelines, our Giving multiplies itself and enables us to pay it forward in countless ways, creating more Giving than Taking in the world.

True Giving, as we will see, is not as simple as just opening our checkbooks and throwing money around.

Guidelines of True Giving

- Giving should be aimed at the recipient's highest-level needs.
- Giving should be done for the other person, not ourselves.
- Giving should have a personal cost for the Giver.
- Giving should be person to person, not institutionalized.
- Giving should challenge the recipient.
- Giving should respect the recipient's highest potential.

I believe when we follow these Guidelines, we clear up all possible confusion. Let's have a look at the Guidelines, one by one…

Giving Should Be Aimed at Higher Needs

For the most part, and whenever possible, Giving should focus on the *higher* needs of our recipients, not on their immediate, low-level needs.

Let's look at our gardener again. If he had realized that Giving away tons of free birdseed on a regular basis was going to attract birdie riff-raff, predators, and disease, he certainly would have thought twice about his particular form of Giving. The fact is, by addressing only the lower and more immediate needs of the songbirds — their need for food — he ignored their higher needs to live in balance and to learn to fend for themselves as nature intended.

We do the same thing when we cater to people's low-level needs, while failing to consider their higher needs, such as:

- The need for independence
- The need for self-respect
- The need to learn job skills and survival skills
- The need to develop character
- The need to grow into Givers themselves

Now, of course, in times of crisis and severe misfortune, immediate, low-level needs must be taken care of. When there's an earthquake, for instance, people need shelter. When there's drought, people need water. When there's famine, people need food. And we often need to address these lower-level needs before we can move on to the higher-level needs.

If our gardener, for example, had found a cluster of starving baby birds in his garden, helping them would have been the humane thing to do. Or if he had been wandering in the forest and decided to spontaneously offer a bit of seed to the wild birds as a Gift, that would have been fine, too. But by instituting a *long-term* Giving arrangement based only on the birds' low-level need for food, he interrupted the fulfillment of their *higher-level* needs to provide for themselves, migrate, and live in harmony with the environment.

We should always keep high-level needs clearly in mind, even as we're helping out with more immediate needs. What may be appropriate to Give in an emergency is not appropriate to Give on a long-term basis.

Fulfilling a person's low-level needs — for food, money, safety, shelter, and sex, for instance — can very quickly become a *barrier* to the fulfillment of their high-level needs. That's because high-level needs typically involve self-sufficiency, maturity, self-respect, and skill development, and *these* needs require that the person fulfill their lower-level needs *for themselves*. See how that works? True Giving, therefore, can sometimes involve literally taking something away from someone, their crutch or dependency, while at the same time trying to remove unfair obstacles to that person's upward growth.

Indiscriminately opening the wallet, on the other hand, is a surefire way to stunt growth.

Giving Should Be Done for the Other Person

A closely related Guideline is that true Giving must be done for the other person, not for us. That means the *other person's* true needs, not ours, must be of primary importance.

Very often, if we examine ourselves honestly, we find we are Giving to someone else in order to feel better about ourselves. That's fine to a certain extent, as Giving *does* and *should* feel good to the Giver, but we have to make sure *our* pleasure and *our* needs are secondary to the true needs of the recipient.

People stuck in the higher Giving numbers of the Dial often have a psychological agenda that underlies their Giving. They Give in order to feel valued and validated, to compensate for a basic lack of self-worth. Their Giving is not really about the recipient; it is about themselves.

As you are doing any act of Giving, ask yourself honestly whether your true motivation is...

- To receive praise and thanks
- To feel important
- To feel superior
- To look good to others
- To enjoy the "buzz" of good feelings your Giving creates
- To trigger a returned favor
- To feel like a noble martyr
- To expiate personal feelings of guilt

If any of these are your main motives in Giving, then you are doing it for yourself and not the other person. What's the problem with that? Well, again, if you're not doing it with the recipient's true *high-level* needs in mind, you will just Give in the easiest, most painless, most immediately rewarding way for *you*. That usually means you'll be playing to the recipient's low-level needs and not their high-level ones that are so much more important.

Giving someone a twenty-dollar bill instantly produces a smile on their face; it's much more enjoyable than taking the time to find out why they're standing on a street corner, day after day, without a job. Buying an alcoholic a drink is a lot more fun than taking her to an AA meeting. Buying your kid a new videogame is easier than taking him to the park and throwing a football with him.

Acts of Giving that scratch *our* itch to Give are rarely the acts the other person truly needs the most. Conversely, Giving that is motivated from genuine concern doesn't always feel good to us in the moment. Quite the contrary, it can be challenging, difficult, and headache inducing.

Which brings us to the next Guideline...

Giving Should Have a Personal Cost for the Giver

One of the surest ways to tell whether your Giving is motivated by the right reasons is that it represents a personal cost to you. In other words, it *doesn't* necessarily feel good. It *isn't* easy or painless. For example, letting your child eat a snack or watch another TV show at bedtime is easy and painless. Reading your child a bedtime story, however, requires *work* on your part, and perhaps means giving up your own TV show and your own personal comfort.

True Giving almost always has a cost to the Giver.

- It is relatively easy for a wealthy businessperson to write a check to a charity organization. It may be much harder for that person to *serve on the board* of the organization, as this will require his time, energy, and management skills.
- It is relatively easy for the superstar heiress to show up at the soup kitchen once a year for a charity photo-op. It might be much harder for her to track down her estranged, drug-addicted brother and try to help him in private.
- It is relatively easy for a rock star to play at a televised charity event (which also, conveniently, helps him promote his new CD). It is probably much harder for him to Give free weekly guitar lessons to a group of musically gifted, low-income kids.

Giving that represents a cost to the Giver has both the best intentions *and* the best results. You know you're not doing it for your own needs. How? Because it's *not* inherently fun and enjoyable. While true Giving may (and often does) turn out to be deeply rewarding in the long run, in the short run, it usually involves effort, attention, risk, sacrifice, and, most of all, *stepping outside your comfort zone*. To be willing to make yourself uncomfortable is the surest sign of pure Giving. Giving that is all about the warm-and-fuzzy feeling of helping, on the other hand, is often pretty superficial and not always aimed at the highest needs of the other. True Giving *costs* the Giver.

Cost is an important factor on the recipient's side as well. Why? Well, it's very important for the recipient to realize that the Giving is costing the Giver something. This makes the Gift personal rather than institutional.

Which leads us to the next Guideline...

Giving Should Be Person to Person, Not Institutionalized

One of the most important and least understood aspects of Giving is that it needs to be personal. Harkening back to our gardener once again, the mistake he made was to "institutionalize" his Giving to the birds. The birds did not have to ask for seed, work for it, or express gratitude for it, so to speak. All they had to do was eat it. This is the same problem we create when we give money and benefits away in an impersonal, "Come and get it" kind of way, either within our families or within our government systems.

We'll talk about this more in an upcoming chapter, but the important point to realize, for now, is that when we take the person-to-person element out of Giving, we rob *both the Giver and the Taker* of crucial aspects of the Give/Take exchange. This is particularly true when the Giving is done involuntarily, as in the case of tax money that is Taken from one citizen and Given to another.

By removing the personal, individualized element, we rob the Giver of both the joy and the responsibility of Giving. The Giver no longer has to think about the needs of the recipient because his Giving has become automatic, involuntary, and routine. Someone else is now handling it, so the Giver no longer has a personal stake in the matter. His caring or compassion is being administered by the system rather than coming from his own heart and from his own sense of social responsibility. As a result, *he* is robbed of the deep joys that come from Giving. Giving is a profound experience that changes the Giver in many ways. When we depersonalize it by making it a systematized routine, the Giver no longer grows from the experience. He no longer needs to develop compassion, wisdom, and boundaries either. His Giving nature is subcontracted out to others, and he is the biggest loser.

But the recipient loses as well. When a person no longer needs to *ask* his fellow man for help but simply fills out a faceless form to prove he is "entitled" to it, he loses all sense of perspective and appreciation. The Gift comes to him without cost and without any sense of reciprocity. He feels no need to pay it back or pay it forward on any level, nor does he feel any sense of humility in asking for the help.

Humility is an extremely important aspect of Taking. I'm not saying a person should feel *shame* for being in need, but whenever one asks one's fellow man to part with his time, effort, or possessions, there should be an appropriate sense of modesty and indebtedness. When we take the personal face out of Giving, we remove the need for such humility. In its place we get arrogance and entitlement. We turn money, food, and medical benefits into water — free commodities for which the recipient has no appreciation.

In effect, we put out bird feeders and ruin the garden for both the birds and the gardener.

Giving Should Challenge the Recipient

When Giving is personal, on the other hand, it *challenges* the recipient. As opposed to the anonymous bird feeder model, the Giving now has a face associated with it. That makes it real and specific. Knowing that there is a real person who is doing the Giving, the recipient does not feel so inclined to milk the privilege. Rather, he is more likely to feel a personal sense of debt and to be challenged to pull himself out of his needy conditions as quickly as possible.

Some of the most effective and creative Gifts are offered in the form of a challenge. Instead of just *handing* the Gift to the recipient, the Giver says, "If you will do *x*, I will Give you *y*." This isn't so the Giver can play power games with the recipient, but rather so the recipient will *value* the Gift and use it to better his life. One famed philanthropist, for example, was known to visit high school freshmen in economically challenged areas. He promised to pay for the college education of any student who maintained an A average throughout his senior year. This creative gift challenged the students to make a sincere and dedicated effort, and the reward only went to those who rose to the challenge, so it was never wasted.

Some philanthropists offer matching challenges to organizations: "You raise *x* number of dollars, and I will match it." This is another way of ensuring the Gift is not just a passive affair.

We can structure rewards with our children in similar ways — not to make them jump through hoops, but to ensure that the Gift serves as a challenge that calls to their higher needs rather than their immediate needs. Something as simple as, "We'll have pizza tonight if you do a great job on your homework" is a challenging Gift.

It's all about rewarding growth, effort, and excellence, as opposed to simply rewarding need. Almost all Gifts — from individuals, corporations, and government agencies — can be structured in such a way as to challenge the recipient to reach for his/her highest potential. But sadly, they're usually not.

Which brings us to the final Guideline...

Giving Should Respect the Recipient's Highest Potential

Any act of true Giving should be offered with deep respect for the recipient or at least for his or her *potential*. When we just hand a person something with no expectations or conditions, there is no respect in that transaction. The hidden message is, "I don't believe you're capable of doing any better than this, so I'm just going to hand you what you're obviously not capable of producing for yourself." True Giving, on the other hand, respects the full human potential of the recipient. It is Given in the spirit of, "I know you're capable of more, and I trust this Gift will help you reach your potential." Gifts Given in this spirit of trust and respect have an enormous power to change people's lives.

One of the most moving scenes in all of literature is found in *Les Miserables* by Victor Hugo. Jean Valjean, the main character, has spent twenty years in prison for stealing a loaf of bread. The experience has jaded and embittered him. One day he manages to escape from prison. He wanders the landscape and is taken in for the night by a priest. Viewing himself as a thief, and with no respect for the kindness or property of others, he awakens before dawn, steals the rectory silver, and sneaks off into the night.

The next day he is caught by the police. They bring him back to the rectory so that the priest can identify him and they can haul him off to prison.

Valjean stands before the priest in shame but is shocked when the priest tells the police that he *gave* Valjean the silver as a Gift. The priest then goes one step further and gives Valjean an *additional* pair of silver candlesticks. "I'm glad you came back, my friend, because you forgot to take these," he tells the thief. The police have no choice but to rescind their charges and leave.

Valjean is confused and tongue-tied. He does not know what to say. The priest then offers him an astonishing challenge. He tells Valjean to keep the silver but to *use* it to become a better man. This Gift is so personal, so powerful, and so challenging that it changes Valjean's life in a single instant. He vows to become a man of good, and he remains true to his word. He uses the silver to buy a button factory, which he proceeds to run as an honest man, creating dozens of jobs for the people in his new village. He becomes a pillar of his community, is elected mayor, and serves honorably in his position.

This story illustrates the power of a person-to-person Gift Given out of deep respect for the receiver's human potential. Imagine if, instead, the priest had simply left his silver outside with a sign on it: "Thieves and Paupers, help yourselves." What change would have transpired then?

Summing Up and Moving Forward

I hope this chapter has helped to clarify what can be a confusing point: how we can become 60/40 Givers without creating a bunch of Takers in our wake. If we follow the Guidelines of *true* Giving, there will be no problem or contradiction. By respecting and challenging the people to whom we Give and by always focusing on their highest needs and highest potential, we can remain in Giving mode the majority of the time without creating a host of dependents around us.

So my simple advice for you is:

- Observe the 60/40 Rule.
- Follow the Guidelines for true Giving.

This formula will transform all of the relationships in your life into more mutually Giving ones.

But of course, first you must weed out the serious Takers in your life and make sure you're correcting any major Give/Take imbalances in your own behavior. Over the next several chapters of the book, we're going to do just that. We're going to look at specific areas of life — work, government, family, friends, marriage — and see where some of the imbalances might lie and what you might do to correct them.

Ready? Then let's march on.

12

Personal Health and Wellbeing

Over the next seven chapters, we're going to take a look at key areas of life and how the Give-and-Take balance can affect us in each. We'll also look at some ways you can make changes if you see signs of trouble. These chapters could really be presented in any order, but it seems logical to start at the most personal level and expand outward, so let's look at the topics in this sequence:

- Your personal health and wellbeing
- Marriage and relationships
- Family and children
- Friends and community
- Business
- Government and Society
- Religion

Again, my goal here is not to present THE answer for finding peace and balance in every area of your life, but to remind you to pay attention to a few of the large icebergs that may be preparing to sink your *Titanic.*

The present chapter will focus on the most personal level of life: your health and wellbeing.

Living in the Hurt Zones Hurts YOU

As we've already discussed, living in 10:10 Zone is the best thing you can do to optimize all of the relationships in your life, but perhaps the *main* reason for living in the 10:10 Zone is to improve the quality of your life itself. Living a balanced life of Give and Take has a direct and immediate effect on your health, your emotional state, and your peace of mind.

On the other hand, living in the Hurt Zone, on the Taking *or* the Giving Side of the Dial, has a major negative effect on all of these factors. One of the main reasons for this is stress. It has been well established by science that constant stress is bad for us — physically, psychologically, emotionally, and spiritually.

A *little* stress can be a healthy motivator and is, in fact, an important part of life. Without stress, most of us wouldn't have reason to get out of bed in the morning or to pull out our A game. We'd coast through life without really challenging ourselves. Stress gives us a kick in the pants and reminds us we need to beef up our strategy or deal with a problem we've been avoiding. Those of us who live in the 10:10 Zone are, in fact, able to effectively use a little stress in a healthy way, to challenge ourselves and to increase our performance.

A *lot* of stress, on the other hand, is debilitating to our health and wellbeing. People who live in the Hurt Zone, on either side of the Dial, tend to live in *chronic* stress. For extreme Givers, this tends to manifest as worry, anxiety, restlessness, or sleeplessness. That's because Givers forever anguish over their loved ones' problems, their own shortcomings, and the state of the world. For extreme Takers, stress presents itself as fear — fear of attack, fear of reprisal, or fear of getting caught.

Stress is only *one* of the health costs of living in the extremes of Give or Take, but it's a biggie.

The Personal Costs of Too Much Taking

People who live in the Hurt Zone — on the Taking side — engage in the greatest paradox of human existence. That is, by being obsessed with what they are getting, they cut themselves off from getting the greatest stuff in human experience: positive emotions, self-respect, a feeling of contribution, a sense of purpose, and the reward of helping one's fellow man. In their zealous attempts to get, they end up eating only the crumbs of life and not the main course.

High-level Takers punish themselves psychologically and, very often, physically as well. Those who retain a trace of morality have trouble living with themselves. Deep down, they know their Taking is anti-life, and they punish themselves for it. Those who have dipped so far into Taking that they no longer have *any* moral compass whatsoever tend to live in fear 24/7, running from the effects of the damage they have done, so they punish themselves in their own way, too.

One common way Takers punish themselves is by what they put in their bodies. Yes, we are back to food again! Inveterate Takers dwell in a constant state of negative emotion — fear, anger, desire — and thereby deprive themselves of joy and love. The only way they know how to escape their emotional pain is through self-anesthesia, which often manifests in the form of smoking, drinking, overeating, and taking drugs. As I mentioned earlier, addiction becomes a major danger for Takers for a couple of reasons: (1) Takers don't know how to stop Taking, so they tend to have powerful, nonstop appetites, and (2) Takers don't experience the *natural* good feelings that Giving produces, so they need to find artificial substitutes.

Science now recognizes that one of the benefits we gain physiologically, through Giving is the so-called "Helper's High." This is essentially a release of endorphins that occurs after performing an act of kindness. It is nature's most direct way of saying, "Well done! Now do more of *that*." Takers who are stuck in the Hurt Zone don't get the Helper's High. They have to settle for the Taker's High instead, relying on addictive behaviors and substances. The truth is, while food, booze, sex, gambling, and drugs can't compete with self-respect and love, they're better than nothing.

Hurt-Zone Takers also have to deal with what I call "body conscience." Even if a Taker is consciously unaware of any guilt or remorse over their actions, in most cases their *bodies* are aware, and their bodies are keeping a record. Human beings, after all, are social creatures. The human body, on a deep-down animal level, cares about the wellbeing of the species. It is connected, at an unseen energetic level, to the whole "herd" of humanity, much in the same way that birds in a flock or fish in a school are connected.

I believe the body registers and "remembers" any act that causes pain and harm to the flock or herd. Such acts run contrary to the survival of the species. And just as endorphins are released as a reward for kindness and Giving, the body takes a punishing hit each time we do something that harms or weakens the herd. The form that hit takes depends on the individual, but if you look at a group of lifelong Takers (prisoners, criminals, hoarders, addicts, benefit-junkies, etc.), you won't see gleaming eyes, easy smiles, good muscle tone, and robust complexions. On the contrary, you'll see the cumulative negative health effects of years of selfish actions.

Another way Takers pay a health toll for their Taking is that they often don't get enough exercise. Their constant state of negative emotion makes life feel dull, painful, and unhappy. As a result, there is no motive to take better care of themselves. (Who wants to live longer when life essentially sucks anyway?) Their lack of self-care, in turn, produces more negative energy, which leads to less and less motivation. They get caught in a deadly Catch-22.

On the flipside, there are Takers who are thoroughly *caught up* in bodybuilding and vanity. These people do have enough positive energy to invest in a somewhat healthy pursuit, but they are so identified with their physical bodies that they become narcissists. It's all about looking good on the surface. Unfortunately, because of what's missing beneath that rock-hard six-pack, their lives collapse in crisis when they eventually lose their physical beauty or are forced to cope with injury or illness.

Extreme Takers often suffer fear-induced trauma. Bernie Madoff, the infamous Ponzi scheme architect, for example, had a heart attack in prison, perhaps from the emotional impact of all his Taking. Heart attacks are common among fear-driven people, and fear is the number one emotion on the Taking side of the Dial. They say if you jump out of a plane, you won't have to worry about how the impact will feel because you'll probably die of a heart attack on the way down; similarly, the further you live down the Taking side of the Dial, the greater the danger of literally killing yourself with fear. The adrenalin the body produces to fuel the fight-or-flight response is useful on an emergency basis — such as when facing a rampaging rhino — but it's quite destructive in the long term. It produces, among other things, infectious illnesses, fatigue, sexual disorders, frequent colds, loss of appetite… and the grim list goes on.

The Personal Costs of Too Much Giving

Being out of balance on the *positive* side of the scale also brings its share of health woes. Over-Giving can cause a lack of self-care that is just as extreme as that of high-level Taking, though the reasons behind this self-negligence may be different. Hurt-Zone Givers are often so obsessed with their self-imposed worries and responsibilities that they:

- Burn the candles at both ends
- Fail to get enough R & R
- Don't take sufficient vacations
- Work through weekends
- Deprive themselves of simple pleasures
- Push themselves to exhaustion
- Worry the night away

The positive energy level that high-end Givers exhibit is admirable, up to a point, but then it becomes a fatal flaw. By failing to replenish themselves through good self-care, their lives become unbalanced. Not only do they get stressed out emotionally, but on a physical level their bodies begin to break down from too much output and not enough input. Sports science tells us that exertion *and* recovery are the twin keys to body strength and growth, but obsessive Givers deprive themselves of the recovery part. They are great on the exertion side, but not so much on the healing/restoration side.

Psychologically, Givers may be prone to a "martyr complex." That is, they convince themselves — whether they admit it aloud or not — that they are unsung heroes who always Give and do more than their share. When life fails to award them the medals they feel they deserve, they can plunge into depression.

Depression, which we now know has a biochemical component as well, can affect both Takers and Givers, but it tends to be more of a Giver disorder. The Giver wants to change the world, and when this goal is not achieved and/or is not counterbalanced by some healthy Taking, the Giver can become deeply despondent. The high-level Giver often turns his disappointment *inward* rather than outward, blaming himself for not being able to fix things.

Ulcers and colitis are typical Giver disorders, as these tend to be caused by worry and self-criticism. Anxiety, sleeplessness, and restlessness often occur, too. Hurt-Zone Givers do not willingly accept care from others, so they close themselves off from much of the healing energy that comes from being touched, caressed, and physically cared for. They become walled-off by their unhealthy one-way flow of all Give, no Take.

Health in the 10:10 Zone

Learning to Give *and* Take has immediate positive effects in the area of health and personal wellbeing. In fact, nowhere are the benefits of striking a 10:10 balance more glaringly obvious than in the health arena. A Giving-centered approach to life, balanced by a healthy ability to Take, has some of the following benefits:

- **Pain is lessened.** When we invest our energy in serving, contributing, helping, creating, and producing, we experience substantially less pain than Takers do. As you've probably noticed, pain — both physical and psychological — is at its most extreme in the wee hours of night. Why is that? It's because that's the time we are the most self-absorbed. The moment we awaken, our attention becomes more outer-directed, and pain lessens. The same thing happens relative to Giving and Taking. When you shift your focus away from *yourself*, pain immediately lessens. The more self-absorbed you are, the more pain you generally feel —

physical, mental, emotional, and spiritual. The more other-directed you are, the less bandwidth you have for your own pain and drama. Takers are so wrapped up in themselves that they are virtually always in some form of pain or another.

- **Appreciation and gratitude are magnified.** Giving has the powerful effect of making us appreciate what we already possess. Want to feel gratitude for something? Give it away! Though that may sound absurd to a Taker, Givers know this secret well. Takers always fear they don't have enough. They look at the proverbial cup as half-empty and think, "If I only had *x* dollars more, *then* I'd be happy." (This is true whether they earn $15,000 a year or $350,000.) They don't want to Give anything away because they worry about losing out. Givers, on the other hand, have discovered that when they Give something away — *especially* when they feel they can't afford it — they realize how much bounty they already possess. They then feel gratitude, one of the most powerful positive energies on Earth. Takers live in a gratitude drought, always imagining they don't have enough.
- **Giving activates the positive emotions.** As we discussed in the "Emotions" chapter, the quality of our lives is largely measured by the emotions we feel. If you live in a tarpaper shack with no running water but feel love and joy most of the time, then you are living a happy, high-quality life. If you live in a ten-bedroom, six-bathroom, oceanfront home but feel mostly envy, fear, and jealousy, then you are living an unhappy, low-quality life. And the simple fact is, Giving stimulates *much* more of the positive range of emotions than Taking does. Yes, Takers get a *blip* of pleasure from a delicious meal, a fun purchase, or a great sexual romp, but it is relatively short lived compared to the long-term positive emotions that a Giving-oriented life produces.
- **Giving boosts the immune system.** Medicine is beginning to realize the powerful effect that emotions have on health. Research is now revealing that the immune system responds to all sorts of charitable

interactions, such as donating, volunteering, and sharing time with others. Something as simple as petting a cat for twenty minutes a day can make nursing home patients more resistant to illness. It seems that when we do things that make other beings feel better, some deep part of us that is connected to all of life responds by making us stronger. On a cellular level, nature rewards positive energy, making us healthier and more immune to illness. New discoveries are being made in this area every day.

- **Giving is an antidote to stress.** Stress can be thought of as the self attacking the self. It is a fear of being unable to cope with the demands of life, a fear that we're going to be overwhelmed and lose everything. Interestingly, the moment we shift our focus to what we're *Giving* rather than what we're getting, stress is drastically reduced. As long as we don't get so carried away with Giving that we forget to replenish ourselves, Giving can be the natural antidote to stress and all of the ill health effects that stress produces. Don't believe me? The next time you wake up in the morning feeling anxious and stressed-out, close your eyes, take a few deep breaths and ask, "How can I *serve* today?" Spend five minutes just contemplating that question in silence, and then act on whatever insights your unconscious mind coughs up. As you throw yourself into your day with this fresh Giving attitude, you'll be surprised to see how easily stress will be pushed to the sidelines and how quickly it will be forgotten. Stress is a feeling of "me against the world." Conversely, Giving makes you feel connected and purposeful.

Which Spiral Do You Want to Be On?

A good balance of Give and Take, with an emphasis on Giving, does much more than improve our health. It also increases our subjective enjoyment of life. It lays the foundation for the most important quality a human life can possess: peace.

When people are asked on their deathbeds what they wish they had done more in their lives, no one answers, "I should have bought more stuff, eaten more junk food, or spent more time worrying about myself." Virtually everyone replies with a Giving answer: "I should have loved more, laughed more, shared more." Giving is the bread of life, as long as it is kept in balance.

Whether we choose a Taking-centric life or a Giving-centric life, we create a self-perpetuating cycle. More Giving leads to more positive emotions and improved health, stamina, and outlook. This, in turn, leads us to be more Giving. The same goes for Taking. Taking gives us negative emotions, which confirm our fears, which ultimately makes us hunker down in our emotional fortress and continue our fearful Taking.

Either way, we create a spiral that leads to more of the same. Which spiral do you want to be on?

13

Marriage and Relationships

After our relationship with ourselves, the next most important relationships, for most of us, are the primary love relationships, such as marriage.

As we plunge into this subject, I must warn you that I don't plan to be overly delicate. When we examine male-female relationships, a whole lot of ancient, primal, lizard-brain stuff comes up, and some of it isn't very pretty. It may be *true*, but it isn't pretty. While we humans have definitely evolved as a species, and while the qualities we seek in a relationship are much more sophisticated than they were even as recently as a hundred years ago, every male-female relationship also contains, deep-down, certain primal characteristics that go back to the caveman days. I plan to be blunt about that, so I hope you don't get offended easily. There is much to be gleaned here, though it may not be easy to hear.

What Men and Women Want

In order to understand Give and Take in sexual relationships, it's important to acknowledge, openly and honestly, what it is that both genders want. In other words, what does the main Give and Take in a relationship *consist of*?

When it comes to our *primary and immediate* needs, I don't think I'm wrong to state the obvious: men want sex and women want security. Of course, relationships have many more facets than that (in fact, if we want *happy* relationships, they

MUST have more facets than that), but again, if we don't look at the big stuff first — the icebergs — we may be pokin' at fly poop again.

Let's go back to our caveman roots. In our meat-eating days, men were the providers. They went out on the hunt and were often away from home all day. When they came home in the evening, all they wanted was a warm cave, a nice meal, and a roll in the hay that didn't involve too much struggle. They wanted relief from the harshness and violence of the world they had to face all day long. They wanted softness and warmth. Gronk may not have admitted this to his buddy Grunk, but that's what he wanted.

Women, on the other hand, wanted protection and security. They also wanted the "extras" that made home a place they *wanted* to stay in all day long. They figured out, very early on, that their sexuality was one thing men valued *very* highly, so they learned to use it. If their man was a good provider, they were nicer to him in the sack, plain and simple. They would *participate* in the act voluntarily rather than fighting him tooth and nail and club.

Underneath all of the complexities of modern society, there is still an element of the above going on in most male-female relationships. We don't like to talk about it, but it's there. Men want sex, and women want security.

When I say men want sex, I mean it as shorthand for a whole list of related things. First of all, men desire a woman's physical beauty. Men, as a rule, are drawn first and foremost to a woman's looks. This attraction can and should deepen into many other areas, but the primary attractor — the catalyst that gets the relationship rolling in the first place — is usually physical attraction. So, women who care for themselves physically and attend to their appearance have an automatic appeal to most men. But beauty extends beyond the body. In most marriages, men expect the woman to be the person who makes the *home and the children* beautiful, too. Men value, rightly or wrongly, someone who can keep a nice home and take care of his other needs. The cooking and homemaking thing is nowhere near as important as the beauty and sexuality thing, but it's an undeniable part of what men want.

Women, on the other hand, want security. When I say *security*, I mean security on many levels — financial security, emotional security, and security from harm. Though looks are important to women, a man's "security quotient" is his true attractor. This is why it is so much more common for younger women to marry older men than vice versa. Older men are more established and confident; they have a higher security quotient. Women like men who are *financially* successful because they can provide nice things to make life comfortable. They are attracted to *strong* men, because, on an animal level, a strong man is capable of protecting their physical safety. Finally, and more recently on the evolutionary scale, they want men with whom they can feel *emotionally* secure. That is one reason intimacy is so important to women. They need to trust a man on a deep level and to know that he has their best interests and the best interests of their offspring at heart. He needs to make her feel emotionally safe. This is achieved through intimacy.

So… men want what they want, and women want what they want. And at a very primitive level, that hasn't changed much in tens of thousands of years. *Society* may have changed, but our primal instincts have not had time to catch up. For this reason, I believe we all need to honestly ask: What is the "currency" that is really being Given and Taken in a relationship? To ignore the primal, caveman stuff because it doesn't fit our self-images or political philosophies is to do a disservice to the relationship.

The BIG question both parties in a relationship need to ask about themselves and their partners, though, is, "Will this relationship be *all* about having our primal needs met, or is there going to be something more?"

Beyond the Superficial

Relationships are not *just* about sex and security, but these *are* main ingredients, whether they're acknowledged or not. We need to strike a good Give and Take on that *primal* level, or we're never going to get very far into the deeper dimensions, where real and lasting satisfaction can be found.

The problem with many relationships is that they don't openly acknowledge the primal stuff, so they don't put it in its proper place. They mistake it for the whole relationship and end up stuck in a superficial trading game that never lets them go deeper.

Let's look at it from both sides, men and women.

MEN

How does a man enter a relationship?

A man sees an attractive woman and, at first, her beauty is all he cares about. He is literally drugged by a churning cauldron of hormones that dull his judgment and make him stupid. (Yes, a woman's beauty is *that* intoxicating to a man.) Her intelligence and energy level factor in, too, albeit to a lesser degree. After all, it's fun to be with someone who laughs at our jokes and has the energy and creativity to do fun things (like have lots of sex).

So if the woman...

- Works out and takes care of her body
- Dresses nicely
- Has good taste
- Is funny, charming, and elegant
- Is sexually attentive

...she might seem to the hormone-drunk man to "have it all." And as long as she looks good and they're having fun, many men do not bother to ask important questions like...

- Does she have a moral compass?
- Is she a good and caring friend?
- Does she have maternal instincts?
- Does she listen to my deepest thoughts?
- Can she share the load in a relationship?

...until it is too late. Why? Because they are too busy focusing on the surface stuff — the qualities that satisfy the primal needs. There's nothing wrong with any of that stuff, of course, but the question is: Does it stop there?

Before committing to marriage, the man needs to look at the woman's Give/Take quotient, beyond the superficial. Is she *obsessed* with her looks and her clothes? Does she care *only* about acquiring nice things? Is it *all* about the superficial stuff to her? Is sex a predictable *quid pro quo* — that is, her sexual generosity is offered in direct proportion to his financial generosity? Is she what I call an "Anita"? ("I need a this, I need a that...") If she is all about her own needs, then she is a Taker, and the man must take notice of this bright red warning flag.

What typically happens with this kind of woman is that once she is married for a few years, she begins to realize she has maxed out her sexual credit card. She decides she has Taken the man for everything she can, so the sex begins to grow less frequent and may even stop completely over time. Anita is now more likely to have an affair than to sleep with her husband; her sexuality has more bargaining power on the other side of the tracks. As a result, the marriage quickly spirals toward disaster.

This scenario can be avoided by a simple look at the Dial during the courtship days. If she's all Take while you're dating, she will be even more Take once the legal papers are signed.

WOMEN

The same caution is offered to women.

During the courtship phase — the mating dance, if you will — women, like men, will tend to notice superficial qualities that play to their own primal needs. For instance, if the man...

- Is strong, attractive, and takes care of himself
- Has a prestigious job
- Owns some nice things
- Is funny, charming, and sophisticated
- Knows how to make romantic gestures
- Has money

...he might seem, to the woman, to be a real *find*. If she does not look beyond her own primal security needs, though, and examine him with a more careful eye, she may well end up married to a Taker. All of the above qualities are fine and good, but she still must ask questions like…

- Is he *obsessed* about working out and his own vanity?
- Does he spend almost all of his time attending to his stuff: his car, his boat, his home?
- Is he a workaholic consumed by office politics and getting ahead on the job?
- Does he seem to work a little too hard at being charming?
- Does he *expect* his generosity and romance to be rewarded by sex?
- Does he become angry, withdrawn, or nasty when his sexual needs aren't being met like clockwork?

A man who is obsessed with materialistic things and/or sex is usually very *need*-focused and very *me*-focused. This kind of man tends to see a woman as a tool to getting his own desires met. He may disguise this very well during the early days, but at the very roots, he is a Taker. He sees the woman as his property, something he pays for via his material generosity. As the relationship develops, this man may very well become abusive, controlling, and manipulative. On the most dangerous level, he may physically threaten and strike the woman. He will also try to control her freedom and monitor her relationships. On a milder level, he may withdraw his emotional availability and financial generosity if he feels he is not getting his needs sufficiently met. Either way, it's all about him and *his* needs.

Again, a critical look at the man and his place on the Dial will prevent many a mistaken "I do."

Taking-Driven Relationships

It is amazing to listen to people who have been married ten or twenty years talk about their spouses. Often, it seems they are talking about a mortal enemy or a distrusted business partner, not an intimate mate. Far too huge a percentage of marriages today either end in divorce or turn into hotbeds of resentment, jealousy, and petty bickering.

What's the reason?

Simply this: both parties are more focused on Take than Give. Marriages in which both parties lean toward the Taking side of the Dial, even many that fall within the 10:10 Zone, tend to become joyless and burdensome affairs that satisfy neither party. They are all about keeping score.

Keeping score is the death of good relationships. Everything becomes a "You scratch my back, I'll scratch yours" arrangement. Women tend to use their sexuality as a bargaining chip; men tend to use their material generosity and emotional availability as the same. The system often becomes very sophisticated, but when you boil it down, it's all about that simple economy.

Because both parties are focused on the getting, they become acutely aware of every little thing they have to Give. They inevitably start to feel they are getting the short end of the stick. Marriage then becomes an endless chain of subtle bargaining moves designed to create more get for each party, and when the get doesn't happen as planned, negativity creeps in. Trust, friendship, kindness, goodwill, mutual support, humor, love, and caring go out the window. Resentment, anger, and strategizing take their place. Both parties start *withholding* all the good stuff that got them into the relationship in the first place.

In such a withholding environment, a relationship has no chance of deepening to a truly satisfying level. As a result, both parties grow resentful that marriage is not Giving them what they had imagined in their romantic fantasies.

Giving-Driven Relationships

A relationship takes an exhilarating turn toward happiness the moment one party decides to throw away the score card and focus on Giving instead. When this simple shift occurs, suddenly all the good things about the relationship — the warmth, the caring, the kindness — come flooding back in. In the vast majority of cases, the sudden change in one partner causes the other partner to react in kind. Your spouse suddenly wants to make *you* happy, too. Almost instantly, the marriage becomes fun and enjoyable again.

It's all about the 60/40 Rule we talked about earlier. It really is that simple. If both parties in every marriage used the 60/40 Rule, we would reduce our divorce rate by 90 percent, have happier children, and put a whole lot of divorce and custody lawyers out of work. I appreciate the simple saying, "Happy wife, happy life," but one can just as easily say, "Happy spouse, happy house." When your partner is happy, *you* feel happy. The score card goes out the window, and you can start enjoying all of those things you were *withholding in order to get your needs met*. All of your needs are met and exceeded through the simple magic of *no longer expecting them* and no longer bargaining for them.

Use the 60/40 Rule across the board in your marriage and see what happens:

- Care more about your partner's physical comfort than your own
- Do 60 percent of the childcare and 60 percent of the errands and chores when you're both home
- Focus more on your partner's sexual pleasure than your own
- Contribute 60 percent of the material/financial stuff
- Listen 60 percent of the time
- Go with your partner's choice — on restaurants, wall paints, TV shows, weekend activities, etc. — 60 percent of the time

The 60/40 Rule is contagious. Once you start using it, your partner will probably start, too. Then both of you will start to realize what marriage is really all about. You will both enjoy the delicious Taking that comes your way precisely because you didn't *angle* for it, and you will both enjoy the inherent benefits of Giving as well. You will enjoy a truly positive partnership that ripens in joy rather than deepens in resentment.

14

Family and Children

Moving outward from our intimate love relationships, we'll now look at family life.

When it comes to raising children, I believe the Dial must play a crucial role. It is important for parents to do an honest assessment of their kids' Give/Take quotient. This is not a step most child-rearing books advocate, nor will you hear it discussed by child psychologists, teachers, educational specialists, or pediatricians. Nevertheless, it is critical. You must look at your kids through the lens of Giver/Taker — not so you can judge them as good or bad, but so you can *take their basic nature into account* in your child-rearing practices.

Most of us are highly resistant to labeling our child as a Taker. That's because we view Takers negatively and Givers positively. We tend not to notice, therefore, the clear signs of a Taker in our child. We write off Taker tendencies as "Kids will be kids," and because *all* kids are Takers to some extent (part of their nature, remember), we often miss the signs legitimately. We have a hard time figuring out when the Taking is a character trait versus a generic trait of childhood development.

Knowing where your child lies on the Dial is an essential part of good parenting.

Recognize Your Kid's Charge

It's helpful, when thinking of your child's Give/Take quotient, to remember that Taking is not bad, in and of itself, nor is Giving purely good. There's no need for value judgments. Again, think in terms of an energy charge. The negative pole of the battery is not *faulty*; it is just negative. By its very design, it is oriented more toward input than output, and that's all.

Similarly, your child has a basic orientation, rooted in his or her DNA. It doesn't help to ignore it or deny it, because then you will fail to appropriately address it. Not all kids are clear Takers or Givers, but many are. You, as the parent, need to recognize which they are. Think about baby boys and girls as an example. Baby boys and baby girls act very differently. Oftentimes, the people who feel this is a sexist statement change their tune when they have their own kids and learn the shocking truth. The differences between boys and girls are stark and obvious.

In much the same way, Giver-kids and Taker-kids are quite different. You can see it pretty clearly *if* you're looking for it *and* are open to it.

One simple way to gauge your child is with food. (It comes down to food again!) Watch the way your child behaves around food, especially when there's a limited supply. At Thanksgiving dinner, it's hard to notice, but see what happens when there's only one pizza and five hungry people. Is your child very motivated to Take more than his share? Notice whether he is generally protective of his food supply, whether he Takes too-large servings, whether he hoards food, and whether he is willing to share his food with a friend or sibling. It's not a sure measure, but it's a good place to start. Here are a few other things to notice…

SIGNS OF A TAKER

The child…

- Literally Takes things away from other kids (active Taker)
- Enjoys having other people — such as Mommy — do things for him/her (passive Taker)

- Gets jealous when other kids play with his/her things
- Ignores others' feelings and concerns
- Takes things s/he doesn't even seem to really want
- Is possessive and has trouble sharing
- Is a "wheeler/dealer"

SIGNS OF A GIVER

The child...

- Cares a great deal about how others are feeling
- Tries to "make things right" with friends and siblings
- Shares easily
- Loves to make Gifts and cards for others
- Seems to lack a possessive sense about toys, snacks, etc.
- Takes genuine delight in others' happiness

One of your central tasks is to identify, without negative judgment, where your child lies on the Dial and make appropriate adjustments. There's a lot you can do that will affect the course of your child's development, but you have to know what you're dealing with from the start. If you allow a high-level Taker to reach his teen years unchallenged, it is unlikely he will ever change. But by the same token, if you recognize his negative charge early on, you can work extra hard at giving him opportunities to learn Giving and to counterbalance his natural tendencies. The Ladder of Life can be a handy guide in this.

Bad Combos

Because nature loves variety, it plays dice with our chromosomes to ensure that our kids are not carbon copies of us. Just because you and your spouse are happy dwellers in the 10:10 Zone (ha, ha!), it doesn't mean your kids will be. Giver parents can have Taker kids and vice versa.

Major family problems can arise when one of the parents is living in the Hurt Zone of the Dial and one of the kids is, too.

If a child, for instance, is a high-end Taker and the parent is a high-end Giver — and no one recognizes this dynamic or puts the proper safeguards in place — that parent is going to get eaten alive. The Giver parent will be highly motivated to provide for the child's needs and to keep the child happy at all times. The Taker child will be highly motivated to *continue* Taking and to *keep* the parent in a Giving posture. Because the parent lacks a Taking perspective, s/he will not realize what is happening and will be unable to set limits on the child. The child, however, *will* recognize this dynamic and will leverage it to make the parent a veritable slave. We've all seen parent-child relationships like this. For the most part, these spoiled kids grow up to be out-of-control Takers who lack the ability to contribute authentically to society.

If at least one of the parents lives in the 10:10 Zone, though, and can see what is happening, that parent can intervene in the situation, putting protections in place and encouraging the mate to gain insight into his/her parenting style. S/he can also make sure a strong set of guidelines is put in place for the child so that his Taking is counterbalanced not only at home, but also at school, in sports, and in other social situations.

At the other extreme, a Taker parent with a Giver child is going to eat *the child* alive. The parent will assume a passive or dependent role, allowing the child to take care of his/her physical needs and emotional needs as well. We've all seen these relationships, too, where the parent's needs come way ahead of the child's. The child is viewed as little more than a pawn whose role in life is to make the parent wealthy, proud, validated, and/or emotionally secure. There's often a sick dimension to such relationships. The child is forced into an adult-like role, filling needs that should be filled by other adults or by the parent herself. In the milder cases, this might create a mama's boy or stage parent. In more extreme cases, it can turn into abuse and incest, sometimes on a long-term basis.

Again, though, if at least one parent is in the 10:10 Zone and spots the tendencies, that parent can make sure the child's true needs are coming first and that nothing inappropriate happens in the family. If *both* parents turn a blind eye to the family dynamics, though, there's going to be a painful descent into the Hurt Zone for everyone involved.

There is usually *some* form of Give/Take imbalance within every family, even if it doesn't rise to an extreme level. To the extent that the family recognizes this and deals with it firmly, lovingly, and with a sense of humor, the family will evolve in a healthy direction. To the extent that they ignore it, the family will get hurt. Families in which there is a great deal of friction between teenagers and parents often have unresolved Give/Take issues buried in their past.

Again, the Dial and the Ladder of Life are good rudders to use when steering your own family. Who are the Givers and who are the Takers in your family? How can you balance the Ladder so it does not tip to either side?

Hardship and Pain Are Not Evil

It's important to realize that only a fully developed, independent adult can develop his/her Giving side. As long as a person is not fully developed, he will have a negative charge and will always be scrambling to get his own needs met. He will be like a half-empty cup with holes in the side. No matter how much water you pour in, it will continue to leak out. He will be a constant Taker. A fully developed, independent person, however, is like a cup that fills up and then overflows with positive Giving.

These days, many kids' Life Ladders are tipping toward the Taking side because we're not allowing them to grow up and achieve independence. One of the main reasons is because we've lost sight of the value that pain and hardship provide. We think: hardship = bad, pain = bad, mistakes = bad. So, as parents, we try to prevent these "bad" things from happening to our kids.

We seem to have forgotten that most of the important lessons *we* have learned in our own lives were a result of unpleasantness, pain, problems, discomfort, and even downright disaster. Just as struggle and hardship create healthy, hardy trees, they also create healthy, hardy human beings.

If we look again at the Ladder of Life, we'll see that healthy parenting begins with providing absolute safety and predictability, but then requires that we pull the safety net away. Many of us seem to have forgotten the latter step. In order for kids to learn independence, they must be given the opportunity to overcome obstacles, threats, and difficulties *on their own.*

Nowadays, a peculiar style of parenting called "helicopter parenting" has developed. Helicopter parents hover around their kids 24/7. They are afraid to let the child out of their sight, lest the child face danger, loneliness, injury, boredom, or the risk of making a bad decision. But children *need* to face hardships and challenges in order to grow.

- **Boredom** gives kids a chance to develop imagination, creativity, and self-direction.
- **Mistakes** teach kids how to do things correctly.
- **Pain, injury, and illness** teach kids strength and build tolerance for higher levels of pain.
- **Loneliness** teaches kids how to reach out to others and make friends.
- **Being picked on** teaches kids how to stand up for themselves.
- **Risk** teaches kids courage and inner fortitude.
- **Falling down** teaches kids how to get back up.
- **Failure** teaches kids new strategies for success.

Modern parents have gotten their roles confused. Many now seem to believe their job is to *prevent* their kids from having "negative" experiences. As a result, they remove all the nutrients on which human souls thrive. The truth is, human beings grow *mainly* as a result of facing adversity and overcoming it. This can be as simple as falling down, over and over, as a toddler. It can be as complex as making the wrong decisions about which friends to hang out with and which school to attend. Kids must be allowed to make their own mistakes and deal with their own adversity. We can't keep them in padded walkers forever, so to speak.

In the East, the lotus flower is a symbol of growth. What's interesting about the lotus flower is that it does not grow in pure, clean water. Put a lotus plant in a crystalline pool and it will quickly die. A clean pool that is free of "problems," you see, is also free of nutrients. Put the same plant in a slimy pond with a deep, murky bottom, and it will grow like crazy and flourish. In fact, the deeper and nastier the muck, the bigger and more beautiful the flower.

The same thing is true for human beings. Those who bloom the most beautifully are those who have learned to convert the "muck" of life into nutrients for growth. Our role as parents is not to coddle kids and *prevent* them from facing the muck; rather, it is to *support* them in *meeting* the muck head on. It is to provide them with a safe place where they can shed some tears, heal from pain, figure out their mistakes, strategize about how to do better, and recommit to trying again. Our role is containment, soothing, and coaching — not prevention.

Yes, it is good to be concerned with our kids' safety, but the media's focus on horrors like child abductions and sexual abuse has created a distorted image of danger. We now imagine we can't let our kids out of our sight for a second without putting their lives on the line. But if we are to have healthy, capable, stable children, we must counterbalance that idea with a reminder that kids *need* to face "danger" on some level. When I think of my own childhood, it is the schoolyard fights, the bicycle accidents, the getting lost in the woods, the adventures, the bored summer days, and the hitting my fingers with a hammer that I remember the most. Dealing with those challenges grew me into the person I am today.

When we over-protect our kids, the subtle message is: "You can't get by without me. You need me because you can't do it on your own." Kids who grow up with this message can't possibly become fully independent. They stay stuck on the left-hand side of the Dial.

15

Friends and Community

As we look outward from our families, it's good to take stock of our whole social network from a Give/Take perspective. "No man is an island," and the importance of other people in our lives should not be underestimated. Other people influence us, and we influence them. And if we want to have a positive effect on the world, it is largely through our social network that we will accomplish it.

I often tell my children that every person you meet in life is an education. The more people you meet, the more of an education you get. One single individual can often teach you more about life than you can learn in an entire four-year college career. If you increase the number of personal encounters you have, you literally make yourself more intelligent. *Quality* of relationships is important, but *quantity* is crucial, too. Just do the math: The more people we meaningfully interact with, the more perspectives we learn.

To have a robust social network means to be keenly aware of your own Give/Take quotient. An introverted, low-energy Giver who keeps to herself and rarely strays outside her little apartment receives a limited education in life. She bases all of her opinions on a very small sampling of people. An extraverted, high-energy Take-and-Giver, however, receives a very diverse education.

Most Take-and-Givers can bond easily with other T&Gers and have an easy time expanding their intelligence. People who live in the Hurt Zones, however, tend to short-circuit their relationships or prevent them from forming in the first place. It's important to recognize where you stand on the Dial. You may not be able to change your essential nature, but by being more *aware* of it, you can work toward opening up your life to more people.

It's also important to assess the *other* people in your life according to where *they* stand on the Dial.

Friendships

Friendships are our most important relationships outside the family. Friendships are vital to a satisfying human life. It has recently been publicized that problems such as homelessness, failed marriages, and health problems can often be traced to the quantity and quality of friendships in a person's life. People who don't have good friends feel unloved, abandoned, and hopeless, and they act accordingly.

Conversely, people who have good friends are happier, healthier, and more productive. Friends *matter*, not only to our personal happiness, but also to our health, productiveness, and creativity.

The upshot of the recent research is that friendships are much more important than we may have previously thought. It turns out that even people who are *three degrees of separation* from us (friends of friends of friends) have a strong influence on our choices and behaviors, even if we never meet those people. Similarly, *our* actions and values can measurably influence people three degrees away from us. Like it or not, we are all part of a vital web of people who strongly affect us and whom we strongly affect.

There are casual friendships and true friendships. Casual friendships are important, but a true friendship offers amazing benefits:

- Someone who values us for who we are, not what they can get from us
- Someone we can confide in
- A shoulder to cry on when things get rough
- A fresh perspective on our problems

- Someone who accepts all of our quirks and eccentricities
- Someone who wants the very best for us
- A kick in the rear when we need to grow
- A sense of shared history
- Someone to care about
- Someone to help us develop our value system

If our friendships are not all they could be, there are two areas we need to look: ourselves and our "friends."

OURSELVES AS FRIENDS

If we find our lives lacking in quality friendships, odds are we are doing something to cause that lack. Either we are choosing to avoid people or people are choosing to avoid us. But why? Hmm…

It's my belief that only Take-and-Givers — folks that live in the 10:10 Zone — are capable of sustaining high-quality friendships. That's because there *has* to be a balance of Give and Take for a real friendship to work. A mix of Give and Take, in fact, is what *defines* a friendship. Friendships, unlike family relationships, are voluntary arrangements. Both parties must be getting something out of the deal.

Takers will have obvious problems maintaining long-term friendships. They might have "buddies" or "chums" or fellow gang members, but they don't usually have *real* friends. Takers often pack together out of mutual need and a shallow sense of companionship. Bullies, for example, will mass in a herd for a sense of security. Womanizers hang out together so they can be each other's wingmen as they strive toward a common goal. Similarly, women who are gold diggers often pack together to practice their digging.

Real friends, though — the kind you know you can call in the middle of the night and they'll come running — require much more effort to find and hang on to. They need to know their devotion is a mutual thing — that *you* value *them* intrinsically and not just because of what they deliver to you. If you are living primarily in the Taking side of the Dial, you are not going to be capable of offering that kind of friendship to another person. Quality friends will avoid you.

If you're too much of a Giver, though, you'll have problems, too. Not only will you attract a lot of Takers intent on exploiting your Giving nature, but even if you do meet some good, balanced T&Gers, they will eventually grow frustrated by having their Gifts go untaken. Unable to share their Giving side with you, they will seek others with whom they can have a more meaningful exchange. You see, good friends *like* to be valued and depended upon. They *expect* their friends to make demands of them. When a friendship doesn't make them stretch and grow, it eventually loses their interest.

Being all-Give in a friendship doesn't work for the Giver either. When we're overly Giving in a friendship, it's not long before that friendship starts to feel like all work, no play. We become burned out. We not only stop participating in *that* friendship, but we even start to tell ourselves that friendships in general are way too much work. Pretty soon, we're living a hermit-like existence, which may be *easy*, but it's also highly unrewarding.

We must be willing to Take something from our friendships in order to experience how mutually rewarding a friendship can be.

Those who live in the Peace Place of the 10:10 Zone truly make the most excellent friends. They Give more than they get, but they know how to Take, too. If you want to increase *your* friendships, I advise you to adopt the 60/40 Rule and make a sincere effort to live in that band of the Dial.

OTHERS AS FRIENDS

When evaluating our friendships, we have to look at the other person, too. We need to take stock of all our friendships and see what they offer to *us*.

Not all friendships deliver the goods.

Many friendships come into our lives due to circumstance. Sometimes these "accidental" friendships can ripen into our most treasured relationships. Other times, those friendships persist simply out of habit or inertia. They can turn into a burden if they are not reexamined from time to time. The old work buddy or the freshman-year college roommate may have seemed like a great guy when you were eighteen, but he may not offer much to your mature, adult self.

Friendships can change over time, too. Casual friendships can deepen into more substantial ones. Deep, old friendships can thin out and become superficial.

It's important to look at *all* friendships, both close and casual, and honestly identify the problematic Takers and Givers. Like tuning your car's engine, this will allow you to harness your energies much more effectively. It doesn't mean you have to *lose* friends (though this might be the result), but it does mean you may have to adjust your expectations. If you are investing too much of your time and energy in a friendship with a Taker, you may need to scale back or challenge that person to change.

One way to identify a Taker is to watch the way a person handles — you guessed it — food, especially in restaurants. It's amazing the way eating habits reveal primal energy.

In a healthy, balanced friendship, both parties will share in the check-paying fairly evenly over time. A Taker, though, will be unable to resist trying to take advantage of others most of the time. If you go out with a group of five friends, the Taker will always order an expensive drink and the priciest item on the menu and will then suggest splitting the bill in five equal shares. If it's a two-person meal and he knows *you're* paying, he will order the lobster. If *he's* paying, he'll suggest you try the "amazing burger." When *you're* buying the beers, he orders Heineken. When *he's* buying the beer, he orders Bud. You know the drill.

You can't make a judgment based on one experience, but if you see this kind of behavior consistently over time, it's a pretty sure sign that the person is a Taker. You might want to think about this person's behavior in other areas of your friendship. Was he sleeping on your sofa for four months when his girlfriend left him? Does he still owe you money on an old loan? Does he charge you for gas when he gives you a ride? Would you hesitate to call him if you had a major personal problem?

Recognizing this person as Taker doesn't mean you have to write him off, but it does mean you need to reevaluate your expectations. If you are expecting true friendship from a Taker, you will get hurt. It is better in the long run to tailor your hopes more realistically. Of course, you can try talking to him about it, and if he decides to work on changing, terrific! But you can't *expect* him to change. You have to be prepared for the croc to remain a croc.

If there is someone who is too *Giving* in one of your friendships, talking might prove more fruitful. You may be able to talk her into accepting more Giving from you. If this doesn't work, you may need to establish some rules in the friendship, such as, "I will only let you drive the kids to soccer this week if you let me drive them next week."

Again, ideal friends are the ones who use the 60/40 Rule with you, and with whom you are able to use the 60/40 Rule in return. Yes, you'll occasionally get into an annoying tussle over the dinner check (each of you trying to pay), but this is a small price to pay for a friendship in which you really do have each other's backs.

Neighbors, Co-Workers, Relatives

Even the non-intimate relationships in our lives can affect us quite a bit, and when extreme Givers or Takers are involved, they can throw life into a tailspin. One thief in the workplace, for example, can put the whole office under a cloud of distrust. One litigious neighbor can make home life a constant headache. One dependent sister-in-law can bring a marriage to its knees.

There are some people we are forced to deal with because of circumstance, and there's nothing we can do about. What we *can* do is, to the greatest extent possible, maximize our dealings with Take-and-Givers, minimize our dealings with Takers, and try to protect and educate the Givers as much as possible.

If there is a Taker in your neighborhood or your extended family, you'll need to put up some boundaries. Protect yourself and your loved ones, and make sure no one's being exploited. Be polite, respectful, and cooperative with the Taker. Always be open to the possibility that s/he will change, but in the meantime, keep your psychological distance.

By the simple act of *identifying* this person as a Taker, you take a major step in the right direction. You say, in effect, "I recognize this person's nature, and I will not make myself vulnerable to his games."

A high-level Taker in the *workplace* can represent a special challenge. This person can actively harm your career, your company, or your income. Takers always try to jockey for advantage, stealing more credit than they deserve and spreading more blame than they should. While a Taker in the *neighborhood* might be just an annoyance, a Taker at work may damage your livelihood.

Identify Takers at work as early as possible. Some possible warning signs are that he or she:

- Complains constantly about pay and benefits
- Coasts on the job
- Is much more concerned with what s/he's being paid than what s/he's contributing
- Misrepresents situations so s/he looks better and/or others look worse
- Takes credit for things s/he didn't do
- Never does anything that's "not in my job description"
- Spreads gossip and rumors
- Views the employer as the enemy
- Refuses to buy into the team vision

On the mild side, Takers can be a drag to work with. On the extreme side, they can steal our work, damage our reputations, and destroy company morale.

Once you identify a Taker on the job, you need to decide whether the Taking is serious enough that you need to report it to your superiors. If so, do it in a cautious and unemotional way. Report only what you've seen, not what you've heard. Be specific and honest and let it go. Then take steps to safeguard yourself going forward. Document your own contributions clearly. Create a paper trail whenever possible. Keep communications clear. Always tell your team members and supervisors what projects you're working on so there is little chance that your ideas and your credit can be stolen.

But mainly, continue to be a positive influence yourself. Don't get sucked into negativity or into *fighting someone else's negativity*. Engaging with someone else's negativity only brings *you* into the Hurt Zone. Just put up the needed boundaries, detach emotionally from the Taker's actions, and practice the 60/40 Rule.

We'll talk more about business in general in the next chapter. For now, just remember to practice this simple formula with all of the relationships in your social network:

1. Identify the problem Givers and Takers.
2. Put safeguards/boundaries in place for dealing with those people.
3. Practice the 60/40 Rule.

16

The Business *of Give and Take*

Now we're going to talk about how the Dial relates to business — *doing* business, *working* for businesses, and *owning/managing* businesses.

I'm no economist (thank God!), but as I look around the business landscape, I see a tremendous amount of negative energy sapping our economy and stifling its long-term growth. A Taking mentality dominates business at the investment level, the labor level, and the management level. At the risk of sounding like a Pollyanna, we need to inject more positive energy into business. We need to shift toward Giving-driven enterprise — as workers, as owners, as investors, and as managers. We need to use the 60/40 Rule as a fundamental guideline in the workplace. When we do this, everyone profits.

It's just common sense. Think about it: If we are all playing the negative 40/60 game, focusing mainly on how we can Take from our jobs and businesses, it's obvious from a strictly mathematical point of view that this is unsustainable. The economy cannibalizes itself. If we're all playing the 60/40 game, on the other hand, economic growth takes off. We create a bigger pie for all of us. Playing the 60/40 game means:

- Employees are more concerned with what they can contribute to their companies than what they get back. They are dedicated to producing high-quality products and services. They can proudly tell their children what they do for a living.
- Companies focus mainly on creating value for consumers and build-

ing trusting relationships with employees. Instead of trying to screw the competition, the customer, and their own workforce in order to maximize profit, they put 90 percent of their energy into developing creative ideas, implementing them with integrity, and rewarding team members for their contributions.

- Investors are dedicated to *growing* businesses, not destroying them for short-term profit. Instead of squeezing good companies out of business to make money, investors strive to help good businesses become *great* businesses.
- Business, in general, is focused on creating value *for the world*, not just sapping its resources. The goal of every business is to make the world a better place, not a poorer, dirtier, nastier, or more dishonest one.

Again, applying the 60/40 Rule may sound simplistic, but I think its very simplicity is what makes it useful. After all, clever economists, stock analysts, and politicians can convince us of anything. They can manipulate statistics to prove that up is really down and that a cow is really a goat. The economy is too complex for the average person — even the average *economist* — to understand. If you want to screw someone in business, you can always find some theory that will help you rationalize why it's a good thing to do, even if your gut knows it's wrong.

But if you really want to know the *right* thing to do, just view the situation from a Give/Take perspective. The simple question in all business transactions becomes this: "Am I more focused on *bringing* something to the table or on snatching something away from the table when no one is looking?"

You *always* know the answer to that question, just by looking into your gut and being honest with yourself. The 60/40 Rule is simple, but that's why it works.

Bad Business

I see many shocking and disheartening examples of out-of-control Taking in business today — practices that are dragging our economy down rather than lifting it up. Here are just a few examples off the top of my head:

- **The increase in hedge funds.** Just a few years back, in 1999, there were about 5,000 mutual funds and fewer than 1,000 hedge funds. Now the number of hedge funds equals or exceeds the number of mutual funds. Why is this a problem? Well, mutual funds buy stocks so that stocks can *appreciate*. They hold them long term and use the appreciation to help fund companies. This is a positive investment. Hedge funds, on the other hand, suck the life out of companies by "shorting" their stock and pulling their value down. This is a *hugely* negative strategy. It has literally wrecked economies around the world, including our own. Hedge funds caused oil to rise from $30 to $150 a barrel. They caused the housing market and our entire financial system to collapse through "clever" use of the futures market. Hedge funds are allowed to legally take companies down, through sheer negative energy, which enables a select few individuals to earn billions while destroying everything you and I have worked for: our savings, pension plans, and stock portfolios. And the worst part? The Takers in government have stood by and allowed it to happen simply because their palms have been sufficiently greased.
- **Unethical bidding.** There's a large construction company in my area that routinely outbids all other companies for big contracts. How? By bidding at 10 percent below cost. How can these guys make money when they bid less than cost? Simple: They steal it by using the legal system. They don't pay their subcontractors! Then they tie them up in court for years. Essentially, they lure subcontractors into working for them by giving them a few small jobs and paying them on time. They then ask the subcontractor to do a large job, and suddenly their checkbook freezes up. Knowing that the shelf life of an average subcontractor is five years, they play a numbers game. They keep their subcontractors bogged down in legal actions, knowing that most of them will drop away by attrition. These guys own big yachts and present themselves as pillars of the business community. They "Give" to charities and politicians, but in truth, they are just evil Takers who destroy the lives of

countless people. And the really sad part is that their success is creating more and more Takers in the Boston area who are trying to emulate their model.

- **Predatory lawsuits.** The whole idea of using the court system to destroy competitors has become commonplace in business, particularly in Internet commerce. You just need to have more financial resources than the other guy. When a competitor enters the marketplace, you sue that company for infringing on your rights (or some other violation), regardless of whether the suit has merit. Your team of high-paid lawyers then keeps *their* team of lawyers jumping through hoops until the newer, smaller company runs out of money. You drive them out of business by lawyering them to death. There is no justice involved here — just pure, predatory Taking.
- **Supply-choking.** Another lovely practice in today's corporate world is to buy all the suppliers' goods that your competitor relies on. Once you own all his main suppliers, you start lowering your prices, making it impossible for your competitor to remain competitive. You drive him out of business, not because your product is better than his, but because you have a Taker instinct and the resources to buy up all the supplies. A variation of this occurs when a large store buys up all the productivity of a supplying business. They buy 100 percent of the company's products, which gives them immense control over the company and lures the company into growing larger and larger. Then the big buyer starts to demand lower prices. When the supplying company can no longer provide the product at the desired price, the buyer pulls out and switches to another company, leaving the former supplier to starve and die. Then the process starts all over again.

I could name dozens of other predatory practices businesses use to increase their Taking without adding anything positive to the world. It's not just the owners or the management doing this, though. Employees do their own share of Taking to drag the economy down.

Labor "Pains"

If you have not dealt with labor unions, then perhaps you "labor" under the delusion that unions are all about protecting noble workers from the evil schemes of The Man. I know I will lose myself a few friends by pointing this out, but unions are far from the romanticized image of Joe Hill and Woody Guthrie songs. While they may have served a necessary function at one point in history, my experience is that they are little more than legalized Takers' Clubs. I'm not saying everyone who *belongs* to a union is a Taker — not at all — but the institution itself pulls strongly to the left side of the Dial. Originally designed to limit the Taking of owners and managers (supposedly), unions now protect wholesale Taking on the part of their membership.

Here's an example. When I was a young man, I did "time and motion" studies for every trade I performed. I wanted to learn how to be more productive and efficient. The biggest benefit I gained from my studies was in bricklaying. See, a union bricklayer would pick a brick out of a pile on line, grab a trowel-full of mortar, butter the end of the brick, then grab another trowel of mortar, throw it over the line, push the brick in place, tap it, swipe the mortar, tap again, swipe the mortar, then repeat this in a slow, methodical way.

I did it more efficiently. I would position the bricks closer to me, making sure the mortar was perfectly mixed, then bend over and grab the brick and a trowel of mortar *at the same time*, slide the brick into place with one swipe, then bend and pick up another brick and another trowel of mortar, repeating this over and over. By removing four steps and by keeping my body fit and strong, I was able to lay between 1,500 and 2,500 bricks a day. A union bricklayer? Between 300 and 700. Of course, I was being paid by the brick, which motivated me to do more in less time. The union, on the other hand, stifled productivity by setting limits on how many bricks a guy was allowed to lay in a day and, of course, by enforcing minimums on how much he had to be paid.

This is a familiar stance of unions. They seem more motivated to squash productivity than to make advances that might benefit the very industries where they make their living. They shamelessly bite the hand that feeds them. As a result, building costs spiral out of control, putting a damper on new construction and producing fewer jobs for everyone, especially the union members themselves! I don't know about you, but I call that a lose-lose proposition. Imagine, instead, if unions took the attitude: "Let's knock the world's socks off with our skills and productivity!"

There are lots of other ways workers Take from the job: phony and exaggerated Workers' Comp claims, abuse of benefits, outright stealing, non-productivity, frivolous lawsuits, protection of lazy and arrogant employees, etc.

The whole problem seems to boil down to an us-versus-them mentality on both sides of the fence. An adversarial attitude pervades all areas of business — the idea that "If *I'm* going to do well, it must be at *your* expense. You are my enemy, and I am entitled to mistreat you in any way I can because business is business." We see this dynamic *between* businesses, *within* businesses, and in the realm of business ownership.

Yet, if we take the Taking mentality out of business, we all can Take more.

Rooting the Negative Out of Business

One of the most extreme Takers I ever dealt with was a guy I'll call Lester. He epitomized negative energy. He ran a box company, and I did most of his contracting work for about ten years. Every time I saw Lester, he was screaming at someone — an employee, a supplier, or a contractor. He paid his workers poorly and constantly yelled at them to work harder and faster.

Negotiating my fees with him was tons of fun. I always had to let him think I was doing the job at cost. Even so, at the end of every job, he would try to get me to knock off another 5 or 10 percent. Nobody wanted to work with this guy. Not only was he unpleasant, but he screwed people left and right. One day I just flat-out asked him, "Lester, why are you such a pr*ck all the time?"

His answer was, "If I'm not being a pr*ck, I'm not doing my job."

Wow, that said it all. At least the man was honest!

Eventually Lester went bankrupt, lost his health and his marriage, and ended up a pathetic old loner. He was a perfect example of the misguided idea that cut-throat Taking is what makes business tick. A lot of people seem to believe this, and I'm not sure why. It's pure negative energy.

A positive approach works so much better — for everyone. There are two simple practices I use to remove negativity from business dealings and replace it with cooperation and positivity:

1. Practice the art of diplomacy.
2. Be a solution, not a problem.

This isn't rocket science, but it works.

Diplomacy

A little diplomacy goes a very long way in the workplace, yet it seems to be a forgotten art. I define *diplomacy* as the art of letting people Give you what you want. When you practice diplomacy, everyone feels honored and positive. There's no negativity whatsoever, yet you still get your way! Diplomacy, however, is an art that requires being fully in the 10:10 Zone.

Learning diplomacy begins when we are babies and we want Mom to feed us. We experiment with crying vs. turning on the charm in order to get our way. We notice that when we're happy and giggly, Mom seems to want to spend more time with us and the nursing process is more enjoyable for both of us.

But then we realize that if we're *too* happy and giggly, Mom may not know we're hungry. Then again, if we *cry* too much, Mom may not enjoy feeding us and will withdraw some of her Mommy warmth. It's all about striking a balance. Some of us learn this balance early on; others do not.

Givers are not good diplomats. They're easy to deal with, but they don't really get what *they* want. They are primarily interested in avoiding conflict. They are the folks who will walk into a car dealership and pay whatever the salesman asks. Their stance is non-confrontational. They cannot imagine or comprehend that a Taker — or anyone — would actively try to take advantage of them. In a business deal between a Taker and a Giver, the Giver will always lose.

Takers, on the other hand, use bullying tactics like my "buddy" Lester did. They yell, rant, rave, boast authority, insult, belittle, and threaten. And while this may get *some* specific results in the short run, it does not produce overall, long-term benefits. It certainly does not lead to peace for anyone involved, and it has a heavy price tag attached.

I learned a long time ago that a 10:10 approach is the best method of negotiating. Let's say, for example, that you walk onto a worksite and see a heavy steel beam that needs to be placed on top of a couple of supports. There are three guys sitting around, but no one is doing the job.

If you're a Taker, you will yell at the men, call them names, and threaten to have them fired if they don't get their butts in gear. Sure, after your browbeating, the workers will reluctantly lift the beam, but then they'll take a forty-five-minute coffee break the minute you leave the room... and call you names Dr. Seuss never dreamed of. You'll pay a price for your bullying.

If you're a Giver, your approach might be to *worry* about the job rather than to ask for help. Not wanting to stir up conflict, you may eventually try to lift the beam yourself. In the process, you'll hurt your back and develop stomach ulcers.

If you're a Take-and-Giver, though, you might tell a little joke to the guys, then say, "Hey, it looks like you guys have a lot more muscle than me. This beam needs to go up right away. Tell you what... you lift the beam, and I'll buy the coffee." The result? The beam goes up right away, and the guys feel respected and rewarded — and you can all laugh over coffee. The guys also feel good because they helped someone out; they got a chance to Give. Everyone wins. That, my friend, is diplomacy.

Be a Solution, not a Problem

Another very simple principle you can employ in all business transactions is to be a solution, not a problem. That simply means you think *first* about what you are offering and *second* about what you are demanding in return. Think about what problems you can solve for the other person before you make demands. This is the exact opposite of the way most people negotiate. We've been taught it's best to *demand* first, which immediately *creates* a problem for the other person and reduces the odds of getting what they want.

Give first, get second is a strategy that improves every form of business negotiation, from asking for a raise to buying a car to selling a multinational corporation. You simply think of the deal from the other person's point of view and ask, "What would I want or need if I were in their position? What would make their life or job easier?" Enter every negotiation from this perspective, and think about how you are *solving and/or anticipating the other person's problems.* When someone sees you as a solution, they will usually be willing to Give you a lot more than if they see you as a problem. That's because you don't trigger their defense mechanisms. Rather, you present a win-win scenario. All they need to do is sign on the dotted line.

- If you want a raise, think about some added ways you can bring value to the job before you demand more money.
- If you're selling a product, think of how it genuinely solves the customer's problems.
- If you're making an organizational change, think about the positive benefits it will bring and then "sell" those benefits to your team in a positive way (rather than threatening, "Shape up or ship out!").
- If you're asking someone to do more work for you, think about how you can show your appreciation to that person now and reward them later.

By practicing these simple methods alone, you can revolutionize your own workspace, no matter what business position you're in. Your positivity will ripple outward, changing people's lives in ways you can't even imagine.

I mentioned some disturbing trends in business a few pages back, but there are many encouraging signs on the horizon as well. Corporations and small businesses are starting to learn that you *can* do well by doing good. By using their products and services to actively solve social and environmental problems (for example, Starbucks selling fair-trade coffee or Rent-a-Green-Box making reusable moving boxes out of recycled materials), they are discovering that customers *want* to support Giving choices and are often willing to pay more to do so. In fact, customers are starting to *demand* that Giving and social responsibility be part of a company's business model. Many companies are now donating part of their proceeds to solve global problems, such as Procter & Gamble cleaning up drinking water in underdeveloped nations. Corporations are starting to show us that, with a Give-first attitude, problems *can* be solved efficiently and voluntarily by the private sector, without the need for government force.

Ah, the government! That brings us to our next topic...

17

Government and Society

Now we're going to talk about one of the diciest topics in the book — government and social policy. There's a reason, I suppose, why it's considered bad form to discuss politics with friends and family: It can be a very polarizing topic. As I share my thoughts in this area, I want to assure you that I don't have a partisan agenda. Frankly, when it comes to party politics, I think both of our parties have a lot of explaining to do. Strictly from a common-sense, Give/Take perspective, though, I believe certain ideas and principles *work* for a productive and free society and certain ideas don't, and I have to be honest in pointing this out.

To me, the truth of the ideas comes first, and the politics run a distant second. I don't choose a political party and then proceed to rationalize everything they do like so many talk-show hosts or columnists. I think about ideas first and then look for the candidates who best embody them, regardless of party. So, though *you* may categorize my politics in a certain way, I promise you I'm only saying what I truly believe makes sense. I realize it may rub some of you the wrong way, so I offer you my apologies in advance.

I'd like to start this chapter with a little story.

The Fall of Rome — from a T&G Perspective

There once lived a landholder in ancient Italy. His name was Antonius, but we'll call him Tony. Tony was a good guy who worked hard on his land and always provided for his family. Tony was such a good farmer that he began to develop some wealth for himself — not Julius Caesar kind of wealth, but enough to enjoy some good Chianti and a nice vacation in Tuscany every year. He had a beautiful home, a happy family, and a good life. He contributed to the community in countless ways. He gave generously to the village fund that maintained the roads and protected the local citizenry.

Tony was also a charitable man who was always willing to lend a hand to anyone in need. As his reputation for being a Giving type began to spread, people came to him for help.

After one particularly terrible crop season, many of the villagers were short on food, so a group of them came to Tony, humbly asking him for assistance. Seeing their hungry children, Tony immediately Gave them bushels of grain, baskets of fruit, and jugs of wine.

It was hard for the people to ask for help from their neighbor, and they were very grateful for Tony's generosity. "How can we repay you?" they asked.

"You can come join me in working my land," Tony said. "I will teach you all the tricks of farming that I know. You can keep most of what you grow, but I'll keep a little, too. After a while, if you have learned your lessons well, I will Give you your own plot of land, and it will be yours to farm forever."

Most of the villagers quickly agreed to this proposal. After all, they were hard workers who had simply run into a stretch of bad luck. They were eager to learn how to farm as well as Tony; someday, they hoped to be as wealthy and successful as he was. They knew an opportunity when they saw one.

Tony's farm became a beehive of activity. Crops were popping up everywhere, and everyone was busy and happy. Tony eagerly taught the people the tricks of his trade, and the people were equally hungry to learn. They worked hard but were living better than ever.

Tony was building his wealth. He continued to work very hard himself, too, so that he could have a surplus and go on helping others in need. Every night when Tony went to bed, he felt good in his heart about what he had done that day. He loved farming and teaching and helping others.

One day, there came a knock at his villa door. Standing outside was a group of Centurions with swords and spears. They informed Tony that his land was now part of the Roman Empire. "From this day forward, we will be Taking everything you produce on your land. But don't worry, *amico*... we'll give you back an amount *we* decide is appropriate. So if you keep working hard, you should still be able to live a decent life."

"What are you going to do with the wealth you Take from me?" Tony asked, shocked.

"It's expensive to run the Roman government," the head Centurion replied. "We need to fund a lot of programs, like the poorhouses we've set up to manage the hungry."

Tony wasn't happy about this arrangement — not one bit — but he tried to make the best of it.

Before long, some of the villagers stopped showing up to work on his farm. When Tony would go to town, he would see them living in housing provided by the government. This made him feel angry and resentful. Tony began to wonder why he was working so hard just to have his money handed over to someone who wasn't working. He decided to cut back on his farming hours and plant fewer crops. Since the *government* was now helping the poor, Tony decided it was no longer his personal responsibility. He went back to just providing for his own family, and his productivity shrank.

Because the Romans were now collecting less and less from Tony and other landowners like him, they needed to Take a larger and larger percentage of what Tony produced. The more they Took, the less Tony had to live on, and the less motivated he was to produce.

Finally Tony stopped working altogether. His farm went to seed, and he spent his remaining days bitterly drinking the last of the wine he had stashed away. His only solace was watching Rome fall around him.

Not a happy story, but what went wrong?

When Tony was Giving from his heart, he felt terrific. He was making a direct contribution to his fellow man. His life felt purposeful. Instead of giving away fish, he was teaching people to fish for themselves and, as a result, everyone was profiting, including Tony himself.

The villagers were better off, too, and because they felt a sense of personal indebtedness to Tony, they did not want to Take any more than was strictly necessary. They were even anxious to pay it back in whatever way they could. They were eager to learn Tony's farming skills because they wanted the maximum return on their efforts. Everyone was motivated to produce at a high level.

When the government took over, though, Tony became bitter and resentful. He began to view the needy as his enemies. The needy lost their motivation to work and began to *expect* their basic needs to be met. They began resenting the landowners who had more than they did. They lost the satisfaction of learning new job skills and providing for their own families. They lost their self-respect.

Instead of everyone winning, everyone was now a loser.

Robin Hood-Style Government Just Doesn't Work

The problem with a Robin Hood style of government — Taking from the "rich" and Giving to the "poor" — is that it doesn't work for anyone involved (not to mention there are very few politicians I'd like to see running around in green tights). When government becomes an organ for the redistribution of wealth, the Ladder of Life collapses. We create an out-of-control garden like the one I described earlier in the book. Both the Givers and the Takers lose, and nobody wins except the people running the government — and even *they* eventually lose as well, when there are too few producers Giving too much of their income away and too many recipients getting too many benefits. The numbers become unsustainable, the government collapses, and as for Rome? Well, it burns.

There are many, many, many reasons why a "Take my money and give it to someone else" philosophy of government doesn't work. Here are just a few:

- **It kills the Giving impulse.** As we discussed earlier, the Giving impulse is one of the noblest impulses of humankind, but the moment you introduce *force* to the formula, the Giving impulse fizzles. People become very resentful when they are *required* to Give, because this overwrites the Giving impulse of the heart. Think about something as simple as Giving a compliment. It's enjoyable to praise someone, but the minute a person *asks* for the compliment — "Aren't you going to tell me I look pretty?" — the Giving impulse sours into a feeling of duty. No one wants to be *told* to do something they would normally feel motivated in their heart to do. Forced Giving has no heart in it, and there's no sense of indebtedness from the recipient.
- **It leads to entitlement rather than gratitude.** When people are unable to meet their own survival needs and must turn to their fellow man for help, it's important that they view the help they receive as a Gift or as charity, not as an entitlement. Gifts and charity are Given out of the goodness of the Giver's heart; the Giver has a kind impulse and wants to share something with the recipient in order to create a bond between them. The moment we *institutionalize* Giving, it loses its charitable nature. We introduce the element of *entitlement* — "If you meet criteria A through F, you are *entitled* to the following benefits..." *Legal* entitlement leads to a sense of *personal* entitlement, the idea that the recipient is *owed* the benefit. In such a system, there is no sense of gratitude, and benefits are taken for granted. Even worse, they are *expected.*
- **It creates more Takers.** If something is available freely and easily, people will Take it rather than work for it. That's a simple law of nature, not a value judgment. It's true of every species on Earth. If you put out birdseed, the birds are going to eat it rather than go hunt for it themselves. If you offer a person a choice between a stack of money or a job application, the average person is going to Take the stack of money. I

would, wouldn't you? Whatever amount of "free stuff" we make available as a society, the number of people "needing" that stuff will rise to meet it. If we Gave away 90 percent of our GNP for free, it wouldn't be long before 90 percent of the population was "needy." Conversely, when we stop Giving stuff away, people find a way to get what they need for themselves, maybe by working or starting a small business. Crazy, I know.

- **It removes hardship and struggle.** Taking money that one person earns through hard work or smart investing and handing it to another person who has not worked hard or invested wisely is economically and morally disastrous. It takes *effort* out of the mix and rewards non-productivity and bad decision-making. We need to recognize that hardship and struggle are vital to the human experience. Overcoming obstacles is the way people learn new skills and develop character. Getting a free lunch teaches nothing and destroys motivation. It also erases the consequences of bad decisions. If a fifteen-year-old single mother, for example, were allowed to suffer the natural consequences of her poor choice to become pregnant (harsh as it may sound), she would probably teach her child not to make the same mistake. She might be motivated to work hard and change her destiny. When mistakes are subsidized by the government and given the stamp of validity, though, we end up with fourth-generation welfare recipients. Sorry, but it's true.
- **It creates conflict between the "classes."** When the government steps in and Takes something you would have Given on your own, you become resentful of the recipients instead of eager to help them. Before long, an us-versus-them mentality arises. Givers become angry because their money is being Taken by force and redistributed. They turn their anger on the recipients. The Takers become resentful of the Givers because the Givers still have more stuff than the Takers. The Takers begin to see the government as a tool for extracting more stuff from the

Givers and Giving it to the Takers. They convince themselves this is a just and noble cause.

- **It leads to ever-bigger government.** The moment a benefit is made readily available, people immediately become accustomed to it and resist having it Taken away. (As I write this, there are actual riots happening on the streets of Paris because the government wants to raise the retirement age from sixty to sixty-two. How do you say "boo-hoo" in French?) In order to win elections, politicians must continually promise *more* benefits, not fewer. This leads to more spending, higher taxes, and a government that can only change in one direction: grow larger.
- **It insults our higher nature.** The argument that the Robin Hood advocates make for Taking from the haves and Giving to the have-nots basically comes down to this: People suck. People are miserable, selfish misers who don't care about their fellow man. If they are not *forced* to share their income, the thinking goes, they will keep it all to themselves. But I beg to differ! I see a great deal of evidence to suggest that people are extremely generous when given the opportunity to be so. Americans, in fact, are the most generous people on Earth. Show us a genuine need, and we respond. Always. The minute we see an earthquake, a flood, a fire, or countless other tragedies, we open our wallets and roll up our sleeves to pitch in. I see absolutely no evidence to suggest that if the government let us keep more of our money we would Give less. Rather, I believe quite strongly that we would Give MORE. By putting the generosity back in *our* hands, we would *own* the Giving process personally, and the joy of Giving would spread like wildfire. True, there might not be as much demand for our Giving because people would no longer feel *entitled* to it, but we would meet and exceed whatever true demand there was. I am absolutely convinced of that. We would do it through person-to-person Giving, through creative charities, and

through socially responsible businesses. We can't do that if Robin Hood is swiping all we have to Give before we have a chance to Give it.

Pied Pipers of Politics

Unfortunately, a long time ago, politicians discovered that the easiest way to get votes is to promise people free stuff. They also learned that there are a LOT of Takers out there and that the Takers show up to vote whenever their Taking is threatened. Creating more Takers, therefore, is the surest way to get more votes.

The easiest — and evilest, in my opinion — thing a politician can do is to promise the moon to everyone. It's an *easy* tactic because it will always get you votes. People *want* to hear that free stuff is coming their way, even if they know it doesn't make financial sense. Throughout our history, politician after politician has played the role of Pied Piper by marching through our streets and promising more stuff to more people.

It's an *evil* tactic because every politician knows such a system is financially unsupportable. The numbers just don't add up. A Taker's Utopia sounds good in speeches, but it's impossible to deliver in real life. If we "tax the rich, feed the poor, till there are rich no more," we end up with no more jobs, no more investors, and no more money to lend to people who want to buy houses and start businesses. And in the end, the economy collapses.

Even if we *could* deliver Utopia, it would not be desirable. *Giving* people all of their basic life necessities topples the Ladder of Life. It takes earning out of the picture and stops the human growth process dead in its tracks. It creates a population full of benefit-junkies who look to government to be the solution to all of their problems and the provider for all of their needs.

Why do politicians promise what they know they cannot, and should not, deliver? Because they are Takers themselves. They know their promises are lies, and they know their policies will run the country aground and cause immense suffering in the long run. Nevertheless, they make the easy promises for one simple reason: They are on personal quests for power. They care more about fulfilling their ego needs than helping humanity. They know they can get votes by promising more goodies to more people, so that's what they do. They covet the prestige and power that come with a high-level government position, and they are perfectly happy to throw you and me under the bus to get it. They don't care about you, and they don't care about the country, no matter how earnestly they proclaim that they do. They care about themselves and about staying in power. They see government as their own personal cash cow and their own personal platform for fame and fortune.

Again, I'm not stumping for any political party here, but I have to say that *anyone* who promises Utopian-style solutions is a Taker and a very bad person. Give your vote to such a person at your own peril; they'll be more than happy to Take it. I'm going resist my temptation to talk about specific government officials and to offer specific political advice, but I think you get my general drift.

Okay, now that I've offended half of my beloved readership, let me proceed to offend the other half.

Let's talk some religion!

18

Religion: The Bible According to Joe

Religion has brought a boatload of benefits to mankind, no doubt about it. In fact, one could easily argue that religion has been the most powerful positive force in human history. Religion gives billions of people a sense of purpose and connectedness. Religion helps us to have reverence for life and a sense of sacredness. Religion teaches good morality and high-level virtues. It preserves spiritual writings and rituals for future generations. Religious organizations have collected billions of dollars for charity and have helped to educate our children, preserve our written language, and shape our public policy. Religion has inspired much of the great art, music, literature, and architecture on our planet. Religion gives structure to the vague stirrings of spirituality in our hearts. Good religion is highly positive energy.

One could also argue that religion has been the most destructive force in history. I don't think I'm stepping out on a limb to say that more human damage has been done in the name of religion than for any other reason mankind has conjured up. Misguided religious beliefs have fueled war, conquest, murder, torture, ignorance, destruction, racial conflict, oppression, *re*pression, *sup*pression, and *de*pression. Religious authority has served as a cover for thievery, sexual abuse, extortion, and political manipulation. Religious doctrine has been a dangerous weapon in the hands of big-time Takers since man's first words were uttered.

Takers in religion have had their way for thousands of years, using religion as a personal tool to fatten their own wallets.

In short, religion is a very, very powerful thing, and it can easily throw its weight to either side of the Dial. Historians tell us there have been literally millions of religions throughout human history, when you factor in all the variations of the thirteen major faiths, as well as all the tiny tribal, familial, and local traditions. So how do we tell good religion from junk religion? Even more importantly, how do we tell good religion from *evil* religion?

Well, the answer to that question, of course, is far beyond the scope of this little book (and this little mind), but there is one basic litmus test we *can* perform. It probably won't surprise you when I say it comes down to Give and Take: Does the religion allow its practitioners to enjoy a healthy balance of Give and Take in their lives, or does it push people into the Hurt Zones? Does it support the Ladder of Life or kick it over?

Qualities of a Good Religion

All religions, in my mind, are legitimate and positive as long as they basically reflect the values present on the Giving side of the Dial, while also maintaining a healthy sense of balance. Essentially, a good religion should be all about:

- Peace
- Caring
- Love
- Compassion
- Mutual respect
- Honor
- Honesty
- Commitment
- Truth
- Tolerance

- Thoughtfulness
- Connectedness

But a religion can't be *all* Give. It must keep its practitioners in *balance* if it is to enhance life and lead to peace of mind. Like a good, healthy friendship, a good, healthy religion will include some Give and some Take. It should make challenging demands of its faithful, yes, but it should also bring them deep rewards. *The point of practicing a religion is to improve your life in the here and now*, not in some promised realm you visit only after you die. That means religion must help you live in the Peace Place of the 10:10 Zone on a day-to-day basis. That occurs only through a healthy balance of Give and Take.

What do I mean by Give and Take in religion? Well, I see it this way. The Give part of religion is the stuff *we* are required to do: prayer, charity, morality, sacrifice, and spiritual practices of various sorts. The Take part is the reward we are supposed to get from our faith: peace, meaning, a sense of purpose, and even perhaps a dash of spiritual enlightenment. A religion should both challenge us *and* nurture us in a balanced way. Any religion that throws our lives *out* of balance is problematic.

Qualities of a Bad Religion

Some classic signs of a bad religion are:

- It makes you feel constant guilt.
- It arouses hatred, anger, and suspicion toward nonbelievers.
- It makes you feel fundamentally flawed, sinful, dirty, or unworthy.
- It demands that you do nothing but Give, Give, Give.
- It *adds* stress to your life rather than helps relieve it.
- It requires that you believe things that run counter to your heart and your gut.
- Its leaders live more opulently than its followers and have more freedoms.

- It asks you to believe things that are truly goofy and just don't square with common sense.
- It asks you to override the wisdom of your heart.
- It asks you to commit acts that are harmful to life, including your own.
- Its dogma is considered more important than your personal experience of truth.
- It considers any form of critical questioning to be heresy.
- It is more focused on sin, evil, fear, and punishment than on joy, love, and peace.
- It is more interested in recruiting new members than serving its present members or serving the world.
- It uses threats of eternal damnation to motivate you.
- It asks that you give up everything *in this life* in order to be rewarded in the next.

Bad religions bring darkness, not light, to our lives. Some bad religions are all about Give, Give, Give, and others are all about Take, Take, Take. Either way, bad religions *destroy* balance rather than create it.

Watch Out for Give, Give, Give

Balance, again, is about a healthy *mix* of Give and Take.

While every good religion should focus on doing good deeds and making the world a more Giving place, we need to be very careful about religions that constantly tell us to Give, Give, Give, without allowing us to Take at all.

There are several issues with Give, Give, Give religions.

First of all, we can fall into the trap of Giving so freely that we create bird-feeder-in-the-garden scenarios. "Feed the poor and clothe the hungry" looks good on paper, but we must critically examine whether the charitable Giving we are being asked to do is really in the best interest of the recipients. Giving should generally meet the criteria of true Giving that I described in Chapter 11. It should be aimed at the high-level needs of the recipients and should challenge both the Giver and the receiver. If your religion is telling you to simply Give lots of your money and possessions away to someone else, you need to question this kind of bird-feeder approach. The best charitable organizations are those that teach people *how* to fish, rather than just give fish away. Instead of just offering free stuff, they ask for some form of moral commitment or paying it forward from their recipients.

Another flaw in many religions is that they tell us to Give, Give, Give in order to be like a spiritual figure, such as Jesus Christ. While there is some value in emulating great beings, we have to be careful that we're not trying to hold ourselves to the same standards as those very rare, enlightened souls who live at the highest numbers on the Giving side of the Dial. As I said earlier, true saints live at a level of consciousness that is beyond 99.99999 percent of the population. If you try to Give at the same level as that of a saint — but you are not *living at the consciousness level* of a saint — you will burn yourself out and will always feel inadequate to the task. Life will become an exercise in guilt and self-flagellation. The vast, vast, vast majority of us normal mortals require *balance:* a balance of Give and Take, a balance of effort and rest, and a balance of caring and being cared for. If you are not a saint, trying to *act* like a saint will keep you in the Hurt Zone.

Another danger with religions that ask us to Give, Give, Give is that they are often corrupt. They ask *you* to Give, Give, Give, so *they* can Take, Take, Take. If a religion or its leadership is building wealth at your expense, you can be sure its Give, Give, Give messages have an ulterior motive. If the constant message to practitioners is "You aren't Giving enough!" the religion is throwing people's lives out of balance.

Again, we join religions not to make us feel burned out, guilty, miserable, and broke, but to enrich our lives. Part of that enrichment comes from the Giving we do, and part of it comes from the feelings of peace and connectedness we Take from the religion. One-sided religions ought to be avoided.

Watch out for Take, Take, Take

Of course, that goes for religions that are all about the Take, too. There are still many religions (or branches of religions) in today's world that promote such extreme Taking practices as:

- killing or inflicting violence on nonbelievers
- killing oneself for the "higher good"
- negating the rights of women or people of different races, creeds, and nationalities
- depriving oneself of basic life necessities and freedoms
- sacrificing animals
- hating and berating nonbelievers
- armed conquest

All of these practices, and many others not listed above, involve Taking away the rights, life, health, happiness, and freedoms of others in the name of practicing *your* beliefs. Take, Take, Take religions will urge young men to walk into crowded markets with bombs strapped to their chests or fly airplanes into buildings. They will orchestrate tragedies like the Jonestown and Heaven's Gate debacles.

One troublesome Taking tactic that many (if not most) religions employ is to claim their beliefs are THE truth, the only truth, and nothing but the truth. While it is certainly understandable that a religion would want to assure its faithful that it offers a valid path to follow, caution and balance must be exercised. Exclusive, my-way-or-the-highway thinking can very quickly lead to violence and wholesale Taking. If the followers of a religion *truly believe* their way is the only way, the next logical leap is to try to convert the world. This can lead to all forms of violence and abuse in the name of supposed truth. Look at militant Jihad or the Crusades.

It is crucial that religions show respect to other religions — a little Give and Take. All religions, after all, are vehicles and not destinations. They are all supposed to carry us to the same place, even if they take different routes. When religions insist that we fall in love with the *route* rather than the destination, this leads to all kinds of one-sidedness. However, when religions respect the fact that their common ground is much more important than their differences, they are able to serve mankind in a mutually cooperative way.

Any religion that is all about values and emotions on the Taking side of the Dial is problematic. Some of these religions rely on threats or guilt to get you to get you to do whatever they ask: "If you don't follow all of our rules without question, you will face eternal damnation." Others rely on positive promises to get you to do things that run against every fiber of your instincts: "If you fly this airplane into this building, you will be rewarded with seventy-two virgins in paradise." Many religions are arrogant, violent, manipulative, and hateful — all qualities on the left-hand side of the Dial. You can be sure these religions will throw your life out of balance.

Do As I Say, Not As I Do

One easy way to assess a religion is to look at the way its leaders behave. Do the leaders and officials follow one set of rules while asking their faithful to follow another? Do the leaders encourage Giving while practicing Taking? We have seen many appalling examples of this in history and in recent newspaper accounts.

- How many televangelists (think Jim and Tammy Faye Bakker) have manipulated their followers into donating money to the point of personal hardship, while racking up fat bank accounts and real estate holdings for themselves?
- How many spiritual gurus have preached sexual abstinence while shamelessly seducing their followers?
- How many fundamentalist leaders have told their young men and women to commit horrendous acts of violence, including suicide, while they themselves hide out in safe havens?

- How many religious officials have overlooked predatory sexual abuse within their own ranks, while condemning others for sexual practices that are nonviolent and consensual?
- How many clerics have controlled the populations of entire countries by telling their followers to work like dogs and live like rats while they themselves reside in air-conditioned palaces with servants, gourmet chefs, and HDTVs?
- How many religious leaders in history have preached, "The meek shall inherit the Earth," while using their influence to amass political power and wealth?

It seems to me that spiritual leaders who use the cloak of religion to practice acts of Taking are guilty of a special form of evil. These criminals Take our highest impulses — to Give, to worship, to share, and to embrace spiritual faith — and twist them around to advance their own selfish agendas. There's a lot of this going around; some of it is subtle and some of it is overt. Still, a lot of us are in denial about it. We often rationalize behavior we see with our own eyes simply because it is so egregious we don't want to believe it.

I suggest taking a fresh look at the leadership and hierarchy of your particular faith. Is there any inconsistency between what is being practiced and what is being preached? Be honest with yourself. If the leaders of your faith are allowing themselves privileges that they deny to their own followers, there's a problem. A healthy sign of good spiritual leadership, on the other hand, is that the leaders are living examples of the religion's doctrine and hold themselves to an *even higher* level of commitment and integrity than most followers can possibly emulate.

Your Own Authority

I believe a religion is successful if it helps us assume authority over our own lives rather than placing that authority in the hands of some outside force. Religion should help us become better at making good decisions for ourselves, not at letting someone else pull our strings.

I believe our *hearts* are the greatest source of wisdom we human beings possess. Whenever a religion tells us to ignore the wisdom of our hearts and accept some bizarre dogma, threat, or promise instead, we should be alarmed. Fear is the weapon bad religions use to coax us to override our heart wisdom and march to their drums. Many religions, for example, teach us to fear eternal damnation, to fear losing out on God's grace, or to fear condemnation by church authorities. (Interesting, isn't it, that the term many people apply to true believers is "God-fearing"?) But this fear never totally erases what our hearts are telling us, and whenever there's tension between what we're being *told* to believe and what we believe in our hearts, we live in anxiety rather than peace. We live in the Hurt Zones.

On the other hand, if a religion can help us learn to trust the wisdom of our hearts *even more*, then it allows us to live in peace and integrity. I believe any religion that enables us to live, day to day, in the Peace Place and strengthens the Ladder of Life is a good religion.

Good religions can truly help us attain peace on Earth. Bad religions, on the other hand, make us fly airplanes into buildings.

So that's a quick and, yes, incomplete look at how the Dial can help us can navigate the complexities of life in several key areas — relationships, work, government, religion. You may very well come to different conclusions than I have about such topics as government and religion, but the important thing is that you find balance in *your* life in a way that works for you. As I've said more than once, there's more to life than the Giving and Taking scale, but unless we look at this crucial factor, we may find our lives spiraling out of control in some key area or another. We may miss the icebergs while staring at the whitecaps.

This I *can* say with some assuredness: If you're experiencing anxiety, guilt, fear, depression, or anger in any area of your life, it's almost certain that your Give/Take balance is off somewhere. That's why I heartily encourage you to take a G/T inventory of all key areas of your life. Are you in balance, or is something out of whack?

19

The Rubber Hits the Road

Okay, so I've been yapping for the last eighteen chapters about balancing the Give and Take in your life. Now it's your turn! I'm going to ask you to take a quick Give/Take Inventory of your life. I know, I know... many of you will be tempted to skip this step, but I urge you not to. Doing a Give/Take Inventory is not difficult or complicated, but it *is* important — especially if you're feeling pain or anxiety or *wrongness* in some area(s) of your life and you don't know why.

The reason it's important to be specific and look at each and every area of your life is that denial might be causing you to avoid looking at painful truths. Left to our own devices, we don't look where we don't *want* to look. If I were to ask you, for example, to generally describe the Give and Take balance in your life, you might reply, "It's pretty good," and leave it at that. But if I asked you to look directly at your *marriage* and answer some specific questions about it, the answer might be quite different.

So I'm going to ask you to take a look at your life in several key areas and to do so through two different lenses: (1) Self and (2) Others. In other words, you're going to answer honestly whether you see yourself as mainly a Giver or a Taker in that area, and then you are going to identify the important Giving and Taking influences *outside* of you. Who are the Givers and who are the Takers? How are they affecting you? How is Giving and Taking playing out in this part of your life?

In each area of life, I'll supply some questions to ask yourself to catalyze the thought process. These are not comprehensive questions; they're just some thought triggers and suggestions. Some are direct, others indirect. Some may be appropriate for you, some may not. Take them or leave them as you see fit. You will no doubt have questions of your own as well.

Ready? Well, then, let's take inventory!

Marriage/Love Relationship

Think about the balance of Give and Take in your main love relationship (if you are currently in one or recently have been).

SELF

- Do you frequently offer your mate compliments, gifts, and/or spontaneous acts of kindness? When you Give something to your mate, do you expect something in return?
- Do you find yourself keeping score in your relationship? Do you often think about strategies for getting more of what you want?
- Do you become sullen, angry, withdrawn, or critical when your needs are not being met?
- Do you genuinely feel terrific when you are able to please your mate in some way?
- Do you often do activities *your mate* wants to do, or do you insist on making most of the choices? Are you only comfortable when you're in control?
- In your heart of hearts, do you truly want what is best for your mate, *even when it is inconvenient or costly for you*?
- Do you complain about your mate often or harbor negative thoughts and fantasies about him/her? Do you genuinely *like* him/her? What feeling comes up in your heart, as a rule, when you think of your mate?

OTHER(S)

- Does your mate make incessant demands on you, either subtly or overtly?
- Does s/he seem to like and appreciate you for who you are?
- Is s/he supportive of you in reaching your true potential?
- Is your mate's approach to you generally positive or negative?
- Does your mate routinely use sex or material things as a bargaining chip?
- Does your mate share equally in the chores and maintenance?
- Honestly now... Do you usually look forward to seeing your mate and spending time with him/her, or does it feel like a burden? Why?

Children

If you have children, how are things in the Give/Take department in regards to them?

SELF

- Do you regularly Give your time and attention — not just your material support — to your kids? Are you fully present to them when you do so, or are you usually writing work emails in your head?
- Do you support your child in pursuing his/her unique interests, or do you try to steer him/her into making choices *you* endorse?
- Do you have any family rituals, such as shared meals, that bring your family together? Are you invested in preserving these rituals?
- Do you count on your child to make *you* feel happy/fulfilled/smart?
- Do you bend over backwards to prevent your child from experiencing hardship?
- Do you have trouble saying "No" to your child? Saying "Yes"?

OTHER(S)

- Do your children have you or your mate wrapped around their little fingers?
- Is your child able to share his/her toys, food, and other belongings?
- Does your child seem to prefer having things done *for* him/her?
- Does your child get genuine joy from making others happy?
- Is your child expected to do chores around the house?
- Is your child able to play with other kids in a Give-and-Take manner, or is s/he always the boss or always the subordinate?
- Is your teenager or young adult child contributing to the household in an age-appropriate way?

Parents

How are things in your relationship with your own parents?

SELF

- Do you still depend on your parents for material, financial, and/or emotional support?
- Do you *expect* your parents to share in the raising of your kids? Do you often use them as free babysitters?
- Do you take care of your parents in some ways? Do you do at least as much for them as they do for you?
- Do you visit your parents often? Check in with them? Call them?
- Do your parents know they can count on you?

OTHER(S)

- Do your parents seem overly dependent on you? Do they always seem to be needing or demanding something?

- Do they try to Give you too much? Do they treat you like a child? Do you let them?
- Do your parents try to interfere in your life?
- Do your parents use guilt or other negative emotions to manipulate you or your family members?
- Do your parents hide their true needs from you because they don't want to trouble you?

Friendships

Is there a good Give/Take balance in the friendship realm of your life?

SELF

- Do you have at least one close friend with whom you can share intimate details of your life, or do you have mostly buddies and activity-based friends (bowling friends, book club friends, etc.)?
- Do you have a friend who, if s/he called in the middle of the night, you would run out the door to help?
- Do you do at least half of the contributing in the friendship — paying for meals and activities, doing favors, providing emotional support, etc.?
- Are you able to accept help/support/praise/favors from your friend(s)?
- Are you more comfortable picking up the bill or letting your friend(s) do it?
- Are you able to challenge your friend(s) when they are not living up to their potential, or would you rather keep the friendship light and breezy?

OTHER(S)

- Do any of your friends lean heavily on you? Do any of your friends encourage you to lean heavily on them?

- Do any of your friends order more expensive food and drinks when they know you are paying?
- Do you have friends who are constantly asking for favors/loans/help?
- Which friends do you run to the phone to talk to? Which friends do you let go to voicemail?
- Have you ever been betrayed by a friend? Has this happened more than once?

Social Network and Extended Family

How are things, Take-and-Give-wise, in your extended social circle?

SELF

- Do you think most people would describe you as a Giver or a Taker?
- Do people outside your immediate circle (family and best friends) often call you if they need help? Do you usually Give it?
- Do you do any volunteer work?
- Do you contribute to your community or extended family in any way?
- Are people in your neighborhood or extended network constantly hitting you up for favors? Do you have trouble saying "No"? Do you feel taken advantage of?
- Do you often borrow money, tools, or materials from neighbors and relatives?

OTHER(S)

- Is there anyone in your social network that is constantly in crisis or has a lot of drama in his/her life? Does this person rely on you to help sort it out?
- Is there anyone who, as soon as you see their name on caller ID, you know they're calling to ask a favor?
- Is there someone you always feel you owe?

Workplace and Work Relationships

Does your job generally bring you positive energy or negative energy? What kind of energy do you carry to the job?

SELF

- Do you contribute your skills at a high level? Are you doing a job that only you can do as well as you do it?
- Are you resentful of many things about your job — the pay, the hours, the work, the organization, the people? Do you use that resentment as a justification for withholding your best effort?
- Do you practice Taking types of behaviors on the job, things you would not want to teach your children to do?
- Are you usually *eager* to get to work or full of dread? Do you think this attitude affects your contribution at work?
- Do you honestly believe you are earning your salary and more?
- Have you ever gotten fired or in trouble at work? Has this happened more than once?
- Do you feel you have to be a super-performer and do it all? Can you ask for help, delegate, or say "No" when it's appropriate?

OTHER(S)

- Does your job honor you, respect you, and pay you fairly, or do you feel taken advantage of?
- Is your job *over*paying you for what you produce?
- Is there anyone in the workplace who routinely takes advantage of you?
- Does anyone claim unfair credit for your work and ideas?
- Who are the major Givers and Takers in your workplace? How do they affect you?

Business and Finance

Is there a healthy Give and Take in your money dealings?

SELF

- Do you often borrow money from people you know? *Lend* money to people you know?
- Are you in a lot of debt? Do you have surplus money to invest?
- Do you add value to the world through a business you own or invest in?
- Do you make any of your money by screwing other people or by creating negative energy?
- Is anyone screwing you financially? Is this a pattern in your life?
- Do you feel "all is fair in business"? Do you believe it's okay to mislead, lie to, and manipulate others in order to protect your money interests?
- Have you even been stabbed in the back financially by someone you trusted?
- Is there any pattern of negative business/money experience that tends to repeat itself in your life — going broke, getting robbed, being accused of dishonesty, etc.? What's that all about?
- Do you pay your bills gratefully or resentfully?

OTHER(S)

- Is there anyone in your life who needs to borrow from you a lot? Is there someone you often hit up for loans?
- Is there anyone you consider financially dangerous to you?
- Who are the most generous people you know? Do you feel indebted to them in any way?

Government, Leadership and Society

How's your Dial when it comes to government, politics, and the larger society you live in?

SELF

- Do you vote? Do you do anything else to actively participate in the political process?
- Do you serve in a leadership capacity in any clubs, companies, or organizations? Have you ever served in public office?
- Do you believe it is the government's role to ensure a "fair" distribution of goods and privileges? To alleviate financial inequality? Do you hope and expect that the government will solve most of your problems?
- Do you complain about government a great deal? Do you try to do anything about it?
- Have you ever collected government checks of any kind? Did you feel you were entitled to them? Have you ever misrepresented facts in order to collect benefits from government or any source (insurance, employers, charities, etc.)?
- Do you vote for higher principles or just for whatever policies will benefit you personally right now?

OTHER(S)

- Do you believe you are unfairly burdened by taxes, fees, and government policies? Who do you feel is responsible for this?
- Do you believe you are being punished by the government for your success? Do you feel there are systemic disincentives in place that are holding you back from succeeding more?
- Are there any current political figures you feel promise the moon just to get votes? Do you ever vote for these candidates?

- Are the policies of the candidates you support designed to create more Taking or more Giving within the general population?

Religion

If you practice a religion, do you feel it is creating balance or imbalance in your life?

SELF

- Do you participate meaningfully in your religion? Do you change your behavior based on its teachings, or is it more of a casual thing — you *say* you believe it on Sunday morning, but don't really change the way you act?
- Do you feel exhausted or burned out by what your religion asks of you?
- Do you feel pressured by your religion to Give more than you think you should?
- Do you surrender to your faith or hold back?

OTHER(S)

- On the whole, do you feel your religion brings you peace or causes you guilt, stress, and/or hardship?
- Is your religion consistent with the Ladder of Life?
- Does your religion seem as interested in bringing you peace and joy as it is in making demands of you and collecting your cash?
- Does your religion show any of the signs of a bad religion I listed in Chapter 12? Do its leaders do anything that seems inconsistent with the message they tell their followers?

Health

I mention health last because health is often a reflection — an effect or consequence — of the way we are Giving and Taking in other areas of our lives. Still, it's good to ask some direct health-related questions.

SELF

- Do you take good care of yourself? In what areas are you not doing as well as you should? Diet? Exercise? Sleep? What's that all about?
- Do you have any bad habits that are affecting your health? Addictions?
- When you do have health problems, what kinds of symptoms typically come up for you? Where in your body do you often experience tension, pain, or illness?
- Do you often complain to others about your physical symptoms, or do you keep them to yourself?
- Imagine you agreed to give your doctor a completely honest report on every aspect of your life: your work habits, your diet and exercise patterns, your alcohol consumption, your sleep habits, your love life, your stress level, etc. What changes do you think your doctor would recommend?

OTHER(S)

- Are there people in your life who you feel are affecting your health?
- Does anyone close to you suffer from addictions or avoidable illnesses/injuries? What's that about?
- Are any of *your* habits affecting the health of anyone you love?

Flipping It Around

I hope you have begun to seriously ask yourself these questions and others like them. I hope you're starting to open up an honest dialog with yourself. What are the areas of life in which you know yourself to be a Giver? A Taker? Where are you in good balance, and where are you out of whack?

As you think about those parts of your life that are more Take than Give, I'd like you to imagine, just for a moment, flipping it around. Just close your eyes and picture what it would mean to become a 60/40 Giver in that part of your life.

- Imagine how it would feel to be a grownup in this part of your life.
- Imagine how it would feel to be the person who sets an example for others in this area of life.
- Imagine how it would feel to be someone on whom other people depend in this area of your life.
- Imagine what it would feel like to make an important contribution in this area of your life.
- Imagine being a driver, rather than a passenger, in this area of life.

Does making that kind of change seem overwhelming to you?

Becoming more of a Giver than a Taker in certain areas of your life may seem like a big leap right now, but it may not be as huge a leap as you think. It all starts with an honest acceptance of where you are right now. An honest, nonjudgmental, non-condemning look at the negative energies in your life will do more to set change in motion than any other step you can imagine.

So let's take that crucial step…

20

Acceptance of the Negative

If you're lost in your automobile, what's the first step you must take in order to get where you want to go? You must ascertain and acknowledge where you are right now. Pretending you're *not* lost (guys, do you hear me?) is no help, nor is blaming the weather, the map, the road signs, or your spouse. The *only* step that *is* helpful is opening your eyes, looking around, and saying, "Here's where I am." Once you do that, it's a fairly simple matter of using the correct tools — a map or GPS system or the person at the service station — to point you toward your desired destination.

Before we can change direction in *life*, we also need to accept where we are right now. That may seem like an obvious statement, but I think the biggest obstacle most of us must overcome is to be honest about *where* we are and *who* we are. Why is this so hard, though?

Because, deep down, we hate change. Even when life becomes painful and miserable, we often prefer to *live* with our misery rather than to look ourselves in the eye and change our behavior. We employ all kinds of clever mental techniques in order to avoid looking at where we really are in life.

But if we're going to live life in the Peace Place, we need to set the mental trickery aside and look at where we *really* are right now. By doing your inventory in the last chapter, you have already started that work. If you haven't done that yet, I am going to further encourage you in this chapter.

How We Avoid the Truth

There are four main strategies we use in order to avoid dealing with the truth of where we are right now: denial, distortion, blame, and rationalization. Most of us use a combination of these strategies to avoid looking at our Give/Take quotient in multiple areas of our lives.

DENIAL

When we employ denial, we simply *pretend* things are not the way they are. This is easy for humans because we are natural storytellers. When we don't want to deal with the facts about ourselves, we simply rewrite them! To do this, we use either active or passive denial. *Active denial* means we fudge the facts about our behavior till they fit the story we want to tell. If we don't want to admit, for instance, that we drink more than we should, we tell ourselves and others that we "only have a glass of wine with dinner," when it's really three-quarters of a bottle every night. *Passive denial* means we ignore what we don't want to deal with and hope it will go away. If we're having chest pains, for example, and we don't want to deal with them, we just stop noticing them. We don't talk about them and try to ignore them right out of existence.

When we deny emotions, we pretend not to have feelings we consider ugly or bad. These are typically the emotions on the left-hand side of the Dial. If we choose not to see ourselves as angry, for example, we will convince ourselves we don't feel anger. Whenever any angry impulse arises, we'll stuff it, repress it, and try to pretend it's not there.

DISTORTION

Distortion means we twist the facts *about the world around us* so our own behavior appears to be acceptable. We convince ourselves, for example, that our spouse is having an affair so we can feel justified going out and have one ourselves. Or maybe we tell ourselves that "everyone on the job" fakes sick days, so we can Take an unearned three-day weekend. We change the facts of the situation so our own behavior seems logical and ethical within that context.

Distortion is also a handy way to justify emotions we're not comfortable with. Telling ourselves our spouse is cheating gives us a handy excuse for feeling anger, jealousy, and desire, which we might otherwise deny ourselves.

BLAME

When we use blame as a technique, we acknowledge that our behavior is not ideal, but we make it someone else's fault. How many wife abusers, for example, tell their spouses, "You made me do that"? How many criminals blame their parents, their neighborhoods, or their circumstances for their life of crime? How many poor students blame their teachers, their schools, or their brain chemistry for their lousy grades? Blame allows us to look at a personal flaw with open eyes while avoiding accepting any responsibility for it. "I'm only stealing because I've been cheated!"

Blaming others for our emotions is a common practice in marriages and other relationships. "Yes, I'm angry, but it's *his fault*!"

RATIONALIZATION

To rationalize means to tell ourselves a problem is not really a problem. We convince ourselves our behavior is the only behavior that makes sense, given the circumstances. "In a dog-eat-dog business world, I *have* to spy on my competitors in order to remain competitive," or "My boss underpays me, so I *have* to steal from the company in order to make ends meet. It's only fair." Rationalizing is what politicians do when they're caught in a lie (like when that Utopia they promised you doesn't come to fruition during their term.)

Rationalizing is a way to justify having emotions and behaviors on the left-hand side of the Dial. "If your wife acted like mine, you'd look at other women, too."

We use all of these techniques — and others — in order to avoid looking at our true Give/Take quotient in various areas of our lives. We make it seem to ourselves that we are not being Takers when we are, or we make it seem that our Taking is the only logical response, given the circumstances.

Does the rationalizing work? Not really. When we're alone with ourselves, in the wee hours of morning, we know it's all bull. Give is Give and Take is Take.

These are very distinct primal energies, and we always know the difference between the two, no matter how we try to fool ourselves.

Set Judgment Aside

So how do we change?

The first step — and it's a biggie — is to set judgment aside. After all, the main reason we employ all of the self-fooling techniques above is because we judge ourselves as "bad" for having certain emotions and tendencies. We view these traits as undesirable, so we pretend we don't possess them. It is our harsh judgment of ourselves — even if we don't admit it out loud — that pushes us to deny, distort, blame, and rationalize.

In order to stop fooling ourselves, we need to stop judging ourselves, at least for the moment. If we could just take the judgment out of the picture, at least temporarily, it would help us be more honest and less defended.

Here's a simple truth that can help:

ALL of us have the whole Dial within us (except, perhaps, the extreme high points on the Dial, which are "special cases"). There's no point in judging yourself as better or worse than anyone else, because there's *no one on the planet* who isn't capable of experiencing the full range of human emotions and tendencies. The only thing we *can* exercise control over is how much time we spend at any point on the Dial, and that all begins with being honest about our tendencies.

We can't get anywhere until we accept where we are now. As long as we deny, distort, blame, and rationalize, we are unable to take meaningful action. The moment we fully accept where we are right now, though, we take the reins of our own lives.

The Power of Acceptance

True Acceptance — about anything — is one of the most powerful steps a human being can take. Unfortunately, most of us spend 90 percent of our energy fighting it off. Millions of people live miserable, unfulfilling lives simply because they refuse to accept what IS — that they lost their job, that their child was killed by a drunk driver, or that their spouse stopped loving them five years ago. How often have you heard someone say, almost with a sense of pride, "I refuse to accept…[fill in the blank]"? The reason most of us refuse to accept basic facts of our lives is because we confuse acceptance with approval. We mistakenly think if we accept something bad, that means we're okay with it, but that's not what acceptance means at all.

Acceptance simply means to say, "What is, is." Acceptance means to set judgment aside and call a spade a spade. Judgment can come later, but acceptance is just the act of recognizing where we are right now. Acceptance means looking in the mirror and making factual statements like:

- I've been yelling at my wife and kids at least once a week lately.
- I stole office supplies from my company.
- I drink four drinks a day.
- I desire my best friend's husband, and I've been semi-flirting with him for years.
- Lately, I've been Taking from my friend John but rarely Giving.

Acceptance occurs the moment a prisoner sits up in his cell and says, for the first time in his life, "I killed a man for fifty bucks." No excuses, no denial, no games — just the facts, fully acknowledged.

True acceptance sets powerful wheels of change in motion. It allows us to deal with the reality of our lives, not the story we've been telling ourselves. It allows us to *own* our behavior rather than blaming it on circumstance or on other people. By setting judgment aside and fully accepting our flaws, we're not saying, "I approve of my behavior"; we are, in fact, clearing the way to make real changes, rather than just continuing to play games of blame, denial, and rationalization in our heads.

Accept and Forgive

If you've been honest in your self-inventory, then I'm sure you have noticed some areas of your life where there are imbalances in the Giving and Taking. I encourage you to make some simple, unadorned, factual statements about your own life, similar to those I've listed above. Then I encourage you to take a further step: Add the phrase "I accept that..." before each of them. For example:

- I accept that I've been yelling at my wife and kids at least once a week.
- I accept that I stole office supplies from my company…

Again, this doesn't mean, "I'm cool with my behavior." It only means "I accept full responsibility. I refuse to blame, distort, deny, or rationalize." Notice what happens when you make such a factual, unapologetic statement. You suddenly become clear-eyed about what needs to be done. You start to make changes in your life, almost without conscious effort. The next time you are about to yell at your family, you will find yourself seeking a different form of expression. The next time you are tempted to Take a ream of paper home from the office, you will find yourself reconsidering.

When we know where we stand with our own actions and emotions, we know how we want to act. We don't need to beat ourselves up or play mind games about it; we only need to follow the simple guidance of our hearts.

There's one further step we can take to help with this. We can *forgive* ourselves for everything we've done up until this moment. Forgiveness, like acceptance, doesn't mean you approve of your past bad behavior. It just means you are ready to stop punishing yourself for it and to do something meaningful and positive to change it. To say, "I forgive myself," means simply this: "I'm starting with a fresh slate as of this moment. I am no longer going to invest my emotional energy in feeling angry, disappointed, or ashamed of myself for my Taking (or my over-Giving). I am going to invest my energy in thinking and behaving differently." Forgiveness means flipping the switch from negative energy to positive energy, and it's only when we do this that we *actually start making changes that benefit others* rather than just wallowing in self-hatred and inertia.

Accept where you currently stand on the Dial, forgive yourself, and move on. That's really the message of this whole book in a nutshell.

21

Wrapping Up

I'm a father (of five children, two generations), so I try to be optimistic about the future; it's part of my job description. But I can't help thinking that in many ways, we are headed in the wrong direction as a society. By trying to Give too much to our children and our citizens, we have been creating more and more Takers with each generation. In our misguided zeal to make life safe and fair for everyone — and to collect easy votes — we have been expecting less and less from each citizen and expecting more and more from government and social institutions.

What happens when we, as parents, teachers, and government officials Give too much? The Ladder of Life tips over! We create a bird-feeder mentality in which too much bounty is available with too little effort required. And that's what's happening right now in America and in much of the world. We're seeing our beautiful garden dissolving into a chaotic mess right before our eyes. Too many people have become too comfortable with Taking. They've forgotten how to provide for themselves. And in the process, *they've* lost the most precious gift of all — the growth and development that occurs when people are forced to learn new skills, new attitudes, and new adaptive behaviors.

When parents and governments attempt to provide all things to all people, there's no longer any motivation for people to grow. Just as necessity is the mother of invention, necessity is also the mother of human development. When we *need* to acquire something in order to survive, we develop the skills and attitudes to acquire it. It's that simple. When that same thing is *handed* to us, we *don't* learn the skills. Period.

The risk-free, trouble-free, totally safe world many people envision as Utopia is one devoid of necessity — the necessity to learn, scramble, and adapt in order to survive. Such a world is also devoid of growth, character, virtue, innovation, and strength. A poor world indeed.

That which is Given freely and Taken without strings attached becomes like water — a precious commodity that is no longer valued because it costs almost nothing to get it.

As I write these closing words, the Thanksgiving holiday has just passed, and my mind has been on the importance of appreciation. I'm laughing to myself as I recall a story from a past Thanksgiving that really opened my eyes to the very point I'm making here: People don't appreciate that which they do not earn. Let me share this cautionary tale from the contracting trades...

A Thanksgiving Surprise

About twenty years ago, I was enjoying Thanksgiving Day dinner with my family when my brother-in-law got an emergency call on his beeper (yeah, we used beepers back in the Flintstones days). My brother-in-law is a plumber, and the call was from a housing project in a nearby city. Apparently *all* of the toilets in the entire building were plugged up. All of units in the building also happened to be Section 8, government-subsidized, low-income housing.

My brother-in-law made a few calls and couldn't get anyone to help him on Thanksgiving, so I told him, "What the hell? I'll Give you a hand." I knew enough about plumbing to be his second-in-command. We had just finished dinner, so I said, "We'll go check out the situation, see what we can do, then come back and have our pumpkin pie later."

We took a drive to the apartment complex and arrived on the scene to find the residents outraged and incredulous. "How could they let this happen on

Thanksgiving Day?" they demanded to know, as if the problem was somehow our fault. There was no appreciation whatsoever for our speedy arrival, even on a holiday.

Nevertheless, we immediately headed to the basement. Decked out in boots and raincoat, my brother-in-law proceeded toward the clean-out cap, holding a massive pipe wrench in his hand. Knowing the kind of pressure that might be building up behind that cap, I didn't want to get any closer, so I stood on the basement steps and offered words of encouragement from afar.

He carefully turned the cap once, twice, then BAM! The cap shot off the pipe with enough force to have killed him if it had struck him. What *did* strike him, though, was — you guessed it — a four-inch-thick stream of human excrement shooting from the pipe like Satan's fire hose. It erupted with the force of Mount Crapatoa, nailed him full-force, and knocked him to the floor. Within seconds, he was literally covered from head to toe, squirming beneath the guck like a birthing mudpuppy. He struggled over and over to get to his feet and catch his breath as the Torrent of Turd, the Geyser of Goo, the Deluge of Dumps, knocked him down repeatedly, nearly drowning him in human waste. The expression on his face and in his screams, was a mixture of horror and revulsion like none I have ever witnessed in all my years of industrial mishaps... and I've seen guys lose limbs.

When the fecal eruption finally subsided, my brother-in-law slipped and sloshed to his feet, looking like a human pretzel that had just been dipped in the world's foulest chocolate. Then his jaw fell open, and I saw what had caught his attention. Scattered throughout Lake Shitticaca were at least *twenty chunks of turkey carcass.*

There was only one explanation for this: The residents of the building — and not just one or two of them, either — had been flushing turkey bones down their toilets. We couldn't figure out *how* they had gotten the bones to go down in the first place (plungers must have been involved) but it was clear that the flushed gobbler skeletons were the cause of the stoppage. And the residents were angry with *us* because their holiday had been ruined?

Ask my brother-in-law how much fun he was having on *his* holiday.

No Bones About It, Something's Wrong

As I think back on this infamous family incident — after I stop laughing, of course — a serious question does pop up. Would the residents of that building have flushed turkey carcasses down the toilets of *their own* homes? Would they have done so if they knew *they* would have to pay the plumbers and clean up the mess?

I think you know the answer.

The reason those turkeys went down those toilets was that the residents had no *stake* in the place where they lived — no financial investment, no emotional investment, no sweat equity, and, thus, no appreciation. The government was paying most of their rent and all of their maintenance costs, so who cared? Oh, something else we noticed that day, by the way, was a lot of open windows in the building. Heat was included in the rent, so many of these people were regulating the temperature in their apartments by opening the windows rather than adjusting the thermostat. Would they have done this if they were paying for their own heat? Of course not!

Like birds getting an endless supply of free food, they were content to turn their garden into crap — literally, unfortunately for my brother-in-law.

I'm not saying these were bad people or stupid people. They weren't. They were simply demonstrating human nature. When we are not required to *earn* the things we have, we lose all sense of responsibility and appreciation for them.

When I think about the direction we're headed in as a society, the image of that fateful Thanksgiving-day basement often springs to mind.

Sometimes I think we're all getting covered in crap, worse than my brother-in-law, but it doesn't have to be that way…

Some Final Thoughts

Each of us has enormous power to change the world we live in, just by the way we choose to live. If you and I commit ourselves to living by the 60/40 Rule in every area of our lives, we *can* and *will* turn the ship around, no question about it. That's the amazing thing about Giving: It's contagious. When others see *us* being more positive and productive, they are inspired to raise their own game. They, in turn, inspire others, who then inspire others, and so on and so on. There is no end to the potential ripple effect that one person's positivity can produce.

It all starts with YOU. You can be a Taker or a Giver. Better still, you can live in the Peace Place of the 10:10 Zone — Giving more than you Take, but still Taking enough to encourage Giving to flow from others as well.

One person *can* change the world, and that world-changer can be you. Are you up to the challenge?

Here are a few final thoughts to keep in mind as you ponder the changes you want to make in your own life, family, and career...

EVERY DAY, BE A FOUNTAIN, NOT A DRAIN

Every morning, as you start your day, set aside just fifteen seconds to commit yourself to being of service and Giving fully of yourself. Make a fresh determination to be a positive influence throughout the course of your day. In every encounter you have — from a meeting with your boss to buying a pack of gum at the convenience store — remember that you have the choice to be light or darkness, positivity or negativity, a fountain or a drain.

Be a fountain! Be one who constantly *brings forth* something of value rather than one who drains the value and energy of others.

Renew this commitment at several key points throughout the day. As you're about to enter a meeting, as you're about to answer an email, or as you're about to enter your home after a long day of work, remind yourself that you want to be a fountain, not a drain. Enter each meeting with energy, humor, and at least one fresh idea. Write each email with constructive intentions. Enter your home with a warm greeting for your spouse (and a flower now and then).

The main person who will be rewarded by your daily commitment is you.

YOUR MOOD CAN BE A BLESSING OR A BURDEN

Keep in mind that your mood, even more than your actions, determines your effect on others. Your mood includes your emotions as well as the attitudes and approaches that go along with them. Emotions and attitudes on the Taking side of the Dial are negative energies that tend to drain those around us. People who exhibit these emotional states are high maintenance and a burden to others. Some of these emotions have been discussed already, but a fuller list of draining emotions, moods, and attitudes includes:

- Apathy
- Lethargy
- Withdrawal
- Guilt/Self-hatred
- Depression
- Cynicism
- Coldness/Emotional flatness
- Neediness
- Fault-finding
- Problem-dwelling
- Arrogance
- Resentment
- Bitterness
- Jealousy/Envy
- Entitlement/Complaining
- Vengefulness
- Intense competitiveness
- Rage
- Heaviness
- Fear/Anxiety

These, of course, are just a few. Fountain moods, attitudes, and emotions, on the other hand, are those that bring positive energy to a situation rather than detract from it. These include:

- Love
- Joy
- Cooperation

- Generosity
- Creativity
- Problem-solving
- Encouragement
- Humor
- Caring
- Compassion
- Leading
- Inspiring

As you enter each new section of your day, do a mood check on yourself. Is your current mood likely to be an addition to or a subtraction from the situation you are about to enter? If it's the latter, can you do a quick attitude adjustment? The simple choice to be a plus rather than a minus is how we change our world. We really don't have to do anything more than that. A life full of fountain choices, rather than drain choices, will allow you to end your days in peace and contentment rather than bitterness and regret.

NO ACT OF GIVING IS TOO SMALL

It doesn't matter whether you are the president of a multinational corporation or a street-corner hot dog vendor. If you commit to doing your job every day with generosity of spirit and a desire to spread positive energy, you *will* have a powerful effect on the world. Any act done with love and without expectation is a meaningful act.

Sometimes the smallest actions can have the largest effect. Someone told me recently that she spontaneously decided one day to buy a coffee at Dunkin' Donuts for the guy at the tollbooth she went through every day. She said the man literally burst into tears of gratitude at her small act of kindness. Who knows? Maybe that guy was contemplating suicide. Maybe that cup of coffee changed his attitude and saved his life. Maybe someday he'll have a child who grows up to cure cancer. We never know what ripples even our smallest actions are causing. Keep that thought in mind each time you have an opportunity to choose between being a Giver or a Taker.

"SPIKING" IS OKAY

Though I'm a huge fan of living in the 10:10 Zone, there are times when you will "spike" into the higher numbers on either side of the Dial... and that's okay. In fact, when we're talking about the higher *Giving* numbers, it's more than okay; it's a very good thing. We *should* spend some of our time in the high numbers of the Giving side of the Dial. After all, it's only when people go into these high Giving numbers that the great acts of human generosity occur. So you certainly should not avoid the wonderful highs of Giving, but you should seek balance. Come down to Earth now and then, and be sure to take care of yourself and accept the Giving of others. Strive to *live* in the 10:10 Zone, while spiking into the higher numbers on occasion. Otherwise, you'll find yourself in the Hurt Zone.

It's okay, sometimes, to spike into the high *Taking* numbers, too. Greed, for example, is not necessarily a bad thing. The desire for certain material things may motivate you to start a business that will provide jobs for other people and perform a valuable community service of some kind. Even violence can occasionally be called for. A bully, rapist, or assailant caught in the act of committing his offense might deserve a major smackdown. It might be the best thing in the world for him to receive and for you to deliver. Suspicion and distrust are appropriate in some situations; there are a lot of Takers out there. Lust and desire have their place, too. As long as your temporary spikes into the darkness are *not causing pain and suffering to innocent people*, they have their place in a balanced life.

It's only when your Dial needle is *hanging around* in the Hurt Zone that you need to be concerned.

ACKNOWLEDGE YOUR DARK SIDE

When it comes to our darker tendencies, it's important not to deny them. Again, we *all* have dark sides and negative emotions. It's only when we refuse to acknowledge them that they erupt and cause us trouble. Think of the mild-mannered office employee who suddenly snaps and kills twelve of his co-workers or the homophobic fundamentalist preacher who gets caught with his pants down in a truck stop men's room. If these people had *owned* their feelings rather than pretending they didn't exist, they might have been able to make more conscious choices rather than having their emotions blow up on them and ruin their lives and the lives of others.

I strongly recommend that you make friends with your own dark side, your Taking emotions. Invite them to the table and listen to what they have to say. You don't have to give them run of the house, but you can and should welcome and acknowledge them.

When a strong negative emotion starts to well up, learn to *feel* it rather than push it away. Most of us are afraid of doing this because we are afraid the anger or lust or fear will sweep us away or hurt us, but the emotion itself can never harm us. Remember that! If you feel yourself starting to get angry, just sit with it, feel it, pay attention to how it makes you feel physically, and notice where in your body it occurs. Ask the emotion what it wants to tell you. "Anger, why did you just show up?"

When we allow ourselves to *feel* our emotions without judging them as bad or stuffing them down, a couple of interesting things happen. First of all, we realize the emotion doesn't kill us and, in fact, doesn't even feel that bad. Second, the "negative" emotion passes very quickly.

It is only when we *resist* the emotion that it persists. Judo masters know this principle well. We make our enemies stronger whenever we fight and resist them, Daniel-san! However, when we allow them to freely expend their own energies, they quickly disempower themselves. So it is with negative emotions. When we give them space to exist, to play out, to announce themselves to us, their energies are quickly spent. They have their say and just move on. We are not driven to act on these emotions. *We* remain in control. It's only when we *don't* acknowledge an emotion that it threatens to take us over and make us behave badly — because that's the only way it can get our attention!

Having all of our emotions on both sides of the Dial allows us to become familiar with them and to integrate our Taking side with our Giving side rather than keeping them walled off from one another through psychological tricks.

LOOK FOR BALANCE IN ALL AREAS

Some of us are major Givers at home but Takers in the workplace. Others may be Takers in our businesses but Give a lot of money to charity. It's as if we try to compensate for over-Giving in one part of our lives by over-Taking in some other area, and vice versa. It's a primitive and not-very-effective way to find balance.

It is better to look for balance *within* each part of your life. Instead of compensating for being Taken advantage of at work by coming home and abusing your family, for example, look for balance at work *and also* look for balance in your family. Don't play off one part of your life against another. Try to have a good mix of Give and Take in each separate area: home, work, love relationships, friendships, community, and spiritual life. That's the way of peace.

And finally…

REMEMBER THIS BOOK ONLY APPLIES 95 TO 98 PERCENT OF THE TIME

I want to end with a caution not to try to apply the principles in this book 100 percent of the time. Although I strongly stand behind the ideas I've presented here, I also recognize that we can't apply them across the board.

Some people are born with mental or emotional conditions that prevent them from having any control over their Give/Take quotient. All we can do is offer compassion to these folks. Some people are just too badly hurt or emotionally damaged to be able to change. Again, all we can do is behave compassionately toward them, while also making sure they are not in a position to hurt us. There are also extreme Takers for whom no insight is possible and extreme Givers who may have deeper insights than a simple guide like this can offer. This book does not apply to those folks.

Keep in mind that the ideas presented here are only workable and helpful 95 to 98 percent of the time, but that's still a lot. I firmly believe the vast majority of our relationships and life situations can be dramatically improved by taking a critical look at them through the lens of Give and Take that I've tried to share with you here. And that's exactly what I hope you'll do. I hope you'll use this book as a guide to help you take a deeper look at all of your relationships — with your spouse, your kids, your job, your friends, your neighbors, your elected officials — and after that deeper look, I hope you'll make one of three decisions:

1. Keep the relationship pretty much as it is (while maybe Giving just a little more).

2. Work on the relationship to change and improve it.

3. Let the relationship go and move on.

If, by reading this book, you are able to change or walk away from even one bad relationship or bring into your life even one rewarding relationship, I will consider our work here a raging success.

Remember, there are basically three kinds of people; there always have been and there probably always will be. You can't change that fact, but you *can* change how you respond to it. Good luck in your growth! May *your* Giving meet *my* Giving somewhere we least expect it, and may they multiply each other tenfold!

And now I'd like to sign off with a new word I've coined. I think you'll be hearing a lot more of it in the near future.

Friendesha,
Joe
Friendesha.com

Appendix A

Famous Takers and Givers in History

Here are just a few prominent Givers and Takers from history and from our present era, in no particular order. This is a very subjective and incomplete list, meant only to give you a general idea. If you don't recognize some of the names, look them up (you might be surprised what you'll learn)! Though most Takers will generate a negative reaction and most Givers a positive reaction, this list is not meant to offer a final moral judgment on anyone. Not all Takers are evil; some are just drawn toward acquisition.

Takers		Givers	
Alexander the Great	Napoleon Bonaparte	Moses	Lao Tsu
Genghis Khan	Hannibal	Thomas Jefferson	Albert Einstein
Marquis de Sade	Mehmed Talat	Gautama Buddha	Abraham Lincoln
John Dillinger	Attila the Hun	Florence Nightingale	Elie Wiesel
Julius Caesar	Nero	Muhammad	Ramana Maharshi
Mao Tse Tung	Joseph Mengele	Confucius	Aung San Suu Kyi
Tamerlane	Tariq Bin Ziyad	Sri Aurobindo	Muhammad Yunus
Jesse & Frank James	Joseph Stalin	Joan of Arc	Paul Newman
Adolph Eichmann	Billy the Kid	Abraham	Thomas Edison
Sir Francis Drake	Kublai Khan	Andrew Carnegie	Louis Braille

Takers		Givers	
Mehmed II	Hernando de Soto	Nelson Mandela	Maharishi Mahesh
Adolph Hitler	Ted Kaczynski	Archimedes	Rumi
Juan Ponce de Leon	Ivan Boesky	St. Francis of Assisi	Dorothy Day
Idi Amin	Saddam Hussein	Louis Pasteur	Elizabeth Fry
Charles Keating Jr.	Al Capone	Jesus Christ	Anuradha Koirala
Hernando Cortes	Pol Pot	Plato	Aki Ra
Caligula	Francisco Pizarro	Aristotle	Roy Foster
Albert Fish	Bernard Ebbers	The Dalai Lama	Brad Blauser
Jim Jones	George Soros	Mother Theresa	Bob Geldorf
Qin Shi Huang	John Wayne Gacy	Dr. Jonas Salk	Leonardo da Vinci
Chandragupta II	Osama Bin Laden	George Washington	Bill & Melinda Gates
Philip II of Macedon	John Gotti	Mary Baker Eddy	Mother Meera
William the Conqueror	"Bugsy" Siegel	Desmond Tutu	Meister Eckhart
Bernie Madoff	"Lucky" Luciano	Martin Luther King	Billy Graham
Charlemagne	Ayatollah Khomeini	Albert Schweitzer	Thich Nhat Hanh
Ivan the Terrible	Vlad the Impaler	Mahatma Gandhi	Jorge Munoz
Tomas de Torquemada	Charles Manson	Mata Amritanandamayi	Ralph Waldo Emerson
Benito Mussolini			

Appendix B

Emotions and Attitudes Around the Dial

Below is a list of some of the most common emotions and attitudes on both the left and the right sides of the Dial.

Left Side of Dial		Right Side of Dial	
Apathy	Depression	Joy	Respect
Arrogance	Manipulation	Love	Appreciation
Lethargy	Coldness	Cooperation	Passion
Withdrawal	Cynicism	Hope/Optimism	Generosity
Guilt/Self-hatred	Neediness	Creativity	Problem-solving
Arrogance	Fault-finding	Freedom	Tolerance
Resentment	Jealousy/Envy	Sharing	Humor
Lying	Entitlement	Wisdom	Encouragement
Rage	Vengefulness	Happiness	Compassion
Deception	Martyr complex	Inspiration	Leading
Fear/Anxiety	Bitterness	Acceptance	Courage
Horror	Entitlement	Persuasiveness	Truthfulness/Honesty
Harm	Coercion	Helpfulness	Awe
Fury	Receiving	Self-sacrifice	Euphoria
Violence	Panic	Generosity	Reverence
Sexual Predation	Terrorism	Gratitude	Life-giving
Lust	Sloth	Humility	Commitment

Left Side of Dial		Right Side of Dial	
Gluttony	Anger	Creativity	Comfort
Despair	Grief	Supportiveness	Charity
Bullying	Threatening	Unselfishness	Kindness
Insulting	Belittling	Attentiveness	Fanatical devotion
Abuse	Getting	Responsibility	Total commitment
Gaining		Maturity	Pure love/giving